YOU CAN DO IT!

THE FYD STORY

Morag Rosie MBE

with Stuart R Harrison M.Ed.

First published in 2015 by
TBE Publishing

Copyright 2014 Morag Rosie and Stuart R Harrison

Printed in Great Britain by Ingram Spark, United Kingdom

Cover designed by
Stuart Harrison and Hamish Rosie

Typeset by Farr out Publications, Wokingham, Berkshire

Photographs © as individually credited within book.

ISBN: 978-0-9934473-0-3

Contents

Acknowledgements

We would like to thank minerals4all.com, *Making Good Health Simple*, for sponsoring this book.

We would also like to thank the following for their testimonials, which enabled us to fill in details. Damian Barry, Chris Blum, Jemima Bouy, Fiona Brookes, Jackie Brookes, Evelyn Carter OBE, Ken Carter, Reg Cobb, Yvonne Cobb, Jane Cole, Dr Madeline Collie, Craig Crowley MBE, Susan Daniels OBE, Dr. Hamish Drewry, Roba Drewry, Parveen Dunlin, Morna Elliott, Kathleen Francis, Helen Foulkes, Claire Emma Fox, Lizzie Green, Naomi Guest, Penny Gunn, Charles Herd, Marcel Hirshman, Dennis Hodgkins, Skye Holland, Claire Ingham, Dave Ingham, Clare Ingle, Diane Kenyon, Fleur Leslie, Gavin Lilley, Edna Mathieson, Margaret Moore, Charlotte Moulton-Thomas, Caroline Parker MBE, Stuart Parkinson, Clare Perdomo, Mark Perry, Sarah Playforth, Dr. Tilak Ratnanather, Malcolm Sinclair, Sylvia Simmonds, Roanna Simmons, Sharon Smith, Dr. Hilary Sutherland, Joanne Swinbourne, Marlene Swift, Terry Thompson, James Townsend, Keith Wardle-Peck, John Walker, Richard Weinbaum, Dr. Tyron Woolfe.

The cartoons are the work of FYD volunteer, John Wheeler, taken from the FYD newsletters.

All the photographs come from the FYD archives. And we also acknowledge other sources: Drewry/Rosie family archives, Karen photography, Chris Blum, James Townsend and White House Press Office.

Foreword

Floella Benjamin (FYD)

I was delighted when I received a request from Morag Rosie to write a foreword to this book because I have always admired her incredible work with the charity Friends for the Young Deaf. It was also a pleasure to get to know members of her wonderful family, Hamish, Fiona and Morna.

I am really proud that Morag has decided to put pen to paper and in her true, forthright manner, share the story of her early life and then the life she lead for the greater part, with FYD.

This book has brought back many memories for me; the projects, volunteers, the children and young people who all benefitted from those magnificent sports festivals and art competitions!

In short, Morag's book is unique, it is a deaf mother's story, about her determination to create a better world for her own family and for the thousands of deaf and hearing children and young people who were fortunate enough to encounter this wonderful woman and the charity that she lead for so many years.

You can read about the wonderful legacy that has been created by FYD; so many hundreds of people going ahead and enriching their lives and that of others. I am sure they all repeat Morag's indomitable refrain "You Can Do It!"

This is an important book that you have in your hands. Many of us are concerned about our future generations; especially for those who still have to overcome barriers that are put in their way by society. So, I invite you all to read it, enjoy it and learn from it.

Thank you Morag, it has been a real privilege to be a part of your work.

Keep Smiling,
Baroness Floella Benjamin OBE

Introduction

On the 19th December 2012, I received an email from Stuart Harrison who had just finished reading the story of how Brett Wigortz, a former American swimming pool lifeguard had come to the UK and created Teach First, an educational leadership programme that is now well embedded in our education system. The book had inspired him to contact me and ask if anyone was writing the FYD story and would I be interested in working together with him.

I replied immediately to say how delighted I was to accept his invitation because his email that evening had, at long last, made my dreams come true – to see the philosophy and story of FYD recorded for the benefit of future young deaf people. I knew it was going to be a fun project working with Stuart as he was someone who knew already, through and through, the values of FYD, making it easy to start from scratch with plenty of good material in the form of testimonials from former participants.

I could not wait to get started, but I had to be patient whilst Stuart completed another book he was working on at the time "Same Spirit Different team; The Politicisation of the Deaflympics" which is now in print. But the waiting time, gave me a chance to make a start by bringing my notes together and recalling the defining moments of my life; the people who inspired and influenced me and the people who have long since gone after sowing the seeds.

We hope you enjoy reading this story, which is written from my perspective; it is about a charity for young people that was said to be ahead of its time and something I now refer to as our 40-year pilot project!

So, whether you are coming across Friends for Young Deaf for the very first time, or looking forward to reliving your personal journey as one of our participants, we would like to have your feedback because we want to know not only what you think of the book but how the story and the events that unfolded have impacted on you. We want to know if this book has motivated you to take action and what will you be doing.

You can email us at the following address:
FYDstory@gmail.com

1

Influencing Morag Rosie

For my sister Roba and me, the most influential person in our lives has been our wonderful father James MacLean. When he was two years old, James was sent away to board at Langside School for the Deaf in Glasgow, because his mother Jeannie already had four children to look after and she was married to an alcoholic who struggled to hold onto his job as a salesman. She had already sacrificed her career as a schoolteacher to raise us children and she supplemented the household income by working as a cleaner.

As far as we can tell, James remained at Langside as a full-time boarder, never returning home for the school holidays until he was 16 years old. Langside was to all intents and purposes, his home. During the school holidays he would sit at the windows of the school waiting for the other children to come back, it must have been a lonely existence for someone so young. Fortunately for James, the teachers, who were mostly male, looked after him and some of the other children by keeping them occupied with sports and other activities.

The teachers spotted James's exceptional talent for football and so he was given time off to practice instead of attending classes. The whole school was honoured when James was selected to play for Glasgow Schools against London Schools and then chosen for Scottish School Boys and the St Mirren youth teams. Eventually, he moved classes to be taught by a female teacher who was horrified to find that he lacked the fundamentals of a good education, being practically illiterate and unable to comprehend English grammar. His new teacher stopped his extra-curricular football in order that he could buckle down and catch up on his studies. James was, naturally, immensely frustrated at not being able to play football!.

Another pupil, Alex Lambert seized on the opportunity to collaborate with James and gain from this situation. Alex was almost the opposite of James and was equally frustrated; academically gifted but lacking in footballing skills. The two boys were able to reach a compromise with their teachers; James was to coach Alex at football and in return, Alex would help James to improve his English language. The agreement was that if James made no improvement, he would have to be dropped back a class. James persisted with his studies and managed to maintain his academic performance for the remainder of his schooldays.

Until his death, anyone who visited my father would find a huge dictionary lying on the floor next to where he sat. Ever since the intervention of Alex Lambert, he would not allow himself to ignore any new words he encountered as they passed across his eyes. I still have his last dictionary with me as a reminder of his consistent endeavour.

When he turned 16, James returned home to live with his parents. He had not returned to a happy environment. By now, his mother had become the object of brutal beatings as the worst of her husband's alcoholism began to take hold, as he drank heavily whilst away on sales trips. Grandfather's road trips were times of respite for the family but James was becoming increasingly concerned for the wellbeing of his mother and four siblings. He decided to take it upon himself and confront his father and deal with it once and for all.

He persuaded Grandfather that the best course of action was for him to leave home and never return, whilst James assumed the role at the head of the household. This period of responsibility was short lived when his mother asked him to emigrate with her and his sister to America. He declined the offer and stayed behind alone, once again, to fend for himself in Glasgow.

By now, he had built up a circle of friends who invited him to accompany them on visits to Greenock where they would gather around the bottom of lampposts to meet other Deaf people. Out of curiosity, he decided to join them one evening and find out what it was all about. He discovered that Deaf people congregated under the light of gas lamps, because it was the only way that they could see each other's signs and facial expressions as they communicated in sign language. They had to meet this way because there was no place indoors that they could call their own. When the group discovered that James could write, they begged him to become their correspondent and to help them find a permanent meeting place. James promised that he would do his best to help when the timing was right.

Amongst this group of new acquaintances was Katherine McGilp, with whom James fell in love with at first sight. As a result, Katherine broke off her engagement to a Chief Constable who was based in Campbelltown. This shocked and disappointed Katherine's family as they were hoping that, despite the obvious poor quality of communication between a deaf and hearing person, she would marry a hearing man. But it was eventually James who carried the day and won the hearts of his prospective in-laws.

James continued to excel with his football and was taken on professionally by Cardiff City as the only Deaf player in the team. Before moving to Cardiff, James and Katherine got married. The two years in Cardiff were not altogether a happy time for our mother, who was constantly homesick for her family and the life she had left behind in Greenock. But then, Father picked up an injury that forced is football career to come to an end. There was then no choice, they had to return home to Greenock and it was here that he found work in the shipyards as a joiner. Eight years later, they started a family and my sister, Roba, was born.

Roba remembers an early childhood that was dominated by our deaf mother's

James MacLean during his days with Cardiff City. (Drewry/Rosie family archive)

passionate belief at the time that her first-born actually had normal hearing. But Roba just turned out to be a smart and alert little girl who fooled everyone into thinking that she was fitting in communication-wise. She was enrolled into a local hearing school but, after a while, the teacher discovered that Roba was profoundly deaf and advised my parents that she should be transferred to Garvel School in Greenock, which happened to be directly opposite the family home on the junction of Nelson and Nicholson streets.

Our mother was horrified at the idea of Roba going to that school as she herself was a former pupil who had spent her whole school career there and despite being bright and artistic, she was not educationally stretched at all. So our parents refused to send Roba to Garvel and instead she went to Gateside School for the Deaf in Paisley. Roba travelled there daily with a nurse called Miss Taylor who was also her teacher at the school and who taught her well.

Unfortunately, within two or three years, World War Two broke out and a reluctant Roba was forced to transfer to Garvel School. Miss Taylor went with her, but she was already close to retirement.

Garvel consisted of two small classrooms for the deaf children and when curiosity drove Roba to look at the older children's work, she found herself pointing out their errors and then getting herself beaten up for embarrassing them. One day, after such a beating, she ran out to our grandmother's house nearby. Finding Roba in a bad way, Grandmother took her back to school to speak to the teacher. Later, she explained to Roba that she should not look at other children's work but leave them alone. Ironically, the older children took advantage of Roba's abilities and threatened her with more beatings if she did not help them with their work, so she obliged in order to maintain the peace!

I was born Morag MacLean on 17th July 1938. Unlike my sister and parents, I was born with normal hearing and then became deaf at 10 months old. Greenock suffered very badly during the War because it was the base for the Home Fleet and later one of the main assembly points for the Atlantic Convoys. All the shipyards along the Clyde, just outside Glasgow had become a daily target for the Luftwaffe

Greenock Blitz (Karen photography. Flickr)

bombing raids. The night raids on the 6th and 7th May 1941 became known as the Greenock Blitz, when 300 Luftwaffe bombers attacked the town. Over the two nights; 280 people were killed and over 1,200 injured. From 18,000 homes, nearly 10,000 suffered damage and 1,000 were destroyed outright.

The authorities had decided that all children and non-essential adults, mainly those not essential to the shipbuilding yards, needed to be evacuated to the Scottish countryside for safety. This created a problem for our mother, who did not want to leave Father alone and so she made the very difficult decision to stay behind whilst Roba and I, along with our cousins were evacuated with our aunt and grandmother to Minard, a small village in Argyll & Bute situated on the western shore of Loch Fyne near Lochgilphead.

When I was three years old, I fell ill and contracted Meningitis. I had an infection of the protective membranes that surround my brain and spinal cord that had become inflamed and there was a very high risk of permanent nerve and brain damage. In my day, almost everyone who had the condition died. Today over 30% of bacterial meningitis cases result in some degree of hearing loss, as a side effect of the administration of ototoxic drugs to cure the infection. Everyone was well aware of the seriousness of the situation and hoped that I would not be killed.

When mother received news of my illness, she immediately found her way to Minard by public transport, which was a difficult journey to undertake during wartime. On arrival, she found small pockets of local women standing outside the place where we lived. They had their heads covered by their shawls as they had started to give up any hope for me and they were already praying. My mother told them all to leave so she could give me her full and undivided attention.

But my health deteriorated further and the local doctor took a risk with his own life, to travel the perilous journey into Glasgow in order to get the vital MB tablets that could save my life. Thanks to the valiant effort of the doctor and the excellent nursing care from my family, I survived.

Our retreat in Minard was situated in beautiful countryside with Minard Castle (now a hotel) about one mile to the south – it was a mansion built by the Campbells of Knockuie in the 18th century. I don't recall anything about our time there, but for Roba it was a time of frustration, attending the local hearing school and learning nothing because she could not communicate with anyone. I have no personal memory of the seven years following the illness during which time I was unable to render a simple smile. Yet, one day Roba was overjoyed to catch me smiling and she ran about the house in celebration. Mother cautioned Roba, ordering her to be quiet because she was fearful that I could relapse and revert back to my somber state.

At the end of the war, we had all returned to Greenock and I joined Roba as she returned to Garvel School. Neither of us have a happy memory of our everyday life there because we did not get a good education. The special class for deaf children by then was reduced to a single room and crammed into every available space, were 22 deaf children. The problem for our two teachers was how to plan and deliver a appropriate education for such a large group who ranged from 3 to 16 years of age. It was no wonder our educational development never stood a chance.

This was a great source of frustration for our father who knew, from his own experiences, how essential it was for deaf children to have a basic education if they were to stand any chance of competing with hearing people for work. So, after a full day's shift in the shipyards, he would come straight home most evenings to teach us and help us to improve our reading and English comprehension.

After learning how to incorporate some new words into sentences, I was keen to put them into practice on paper at school. Sadly, my efforts were not recognised by the teachers who were furious, knowing that it was our father and not they, who had taught us the best use of English. Roba told me years later how the teachers made me cross out my work.

The relationship between our family and the school began to deteriorate and life became unbearable, especially for Roba. At the age of 14, she started to feel rebellious about wasting any more time and would stay away from school under various pretexts to the consternation of our poor mother. One day, the headmistress went knocking on our door to find out what Roba's latest illness was. She insisted on talking to Roba in person and she was ushered into her bedroom. She found my sister in bed with the bedclothes pulled up to her chin, apparently she went away satisfied not realizing Roba's little secret; she was fully dressed under the sheets and therefore she was up and about as soon as the coast was clear!

Eventually, with the help of our Aunt and without the knowledge of the school, Roba, with Father's consent, was admitted to the Rudmore College of Dress Design in Glasgow to pursue her dream of becoming a fashion designer. The teachers at school became more suspicious of her absence and it became more and more difficult for me to cover the truth under their frequent questioning about Roba's whereabouts. It took them another month before they discovered the real truth.

Our father was summoned before the Education Committee to explain what was going on. Roba and our aunt Morag (who acted as their interpreter) went with him. My sister recalls how our two teachers sat red-faced throughout the proceedings as Father was given the opportunity to explain how he was using his spare time to teach us at home, in the evenings, and how frustrated he was when comparing the big difference in the standard of our cousin's school work in comparison to Roba's and how he felt she would have been making better progress given the right circumstances. Father argued this case in a statement that demonstrated how he had become an advocate for the local Deaf community:

> The Most Vital Question is affecting the welfare of the Deaf in Education. The standard of Education in Greenock is most elementary and I should like to know if the Deaf of this community would have your support in furthering the standard, deaf children being treated in the same way as normal hearing children. The position is that in Greenock there is only one classroom and 22 children ranging from the ages of 3 to 16 years old, being grouped together there. It is impossible therefore to give each child tuition according to his/her age. An ideal solution would be to have deaf children boarded out in a properly established school for the Deaf where there would be class rooms for the different ages with especially trained teachers (for the Deaf) in charge of such class room.
>
> In Greenock the system is Oral but both oral and manual language should be taught. If those of us here did not know the manual language, how else could we have followed your discourse. We, of the adult deaf, feel that until such time as the question of education for the deaf has the government's serious consideration, deaf children will have a poor chance of taking place in the world as useful citizens.
>
> The second point affecting us deeply is to have our own Institute. Much smaller towns have their own Institution and we should like to know if we have your sympathy in this connection.
>
> The Deaf are equally handicapped with the Blind but their affliction is not so obvious. We feel that if the general public thought of us not in the abstract but as intelligent people striving ourselves in the town as people dependable and capable employees. Would you be willing to help our cause?

After listening to all sides of the debate, the Committee found in favour of our father on the condition that Roba returned to school for one month before being allowed to resume her studies at Rudmore, which was thirty minutes away from home by train. Roba dreaded the thought of returning to the school for the obligatory month but she recalled that it was worth toughing out the humiliating set back to have the chance to resume her studies that *gave me the most cherished memories of learning properly.*

For some time afterwards, I envied my older sister, I felt it was OK for Roba to be able to get away from the school at 14, but for me, life was unfair, there was no slight chance of me having the same opportunity and I had to stay put until I reached 16. I still learnt very little from my time at Garvel and continued to rely heavily on

Father's help in the evenings. I remember how I would be playing outside in the streets with hearing children after school and on his return home from work, Father would throw open the window and whistle to draw the attention of my playmates who would tell me to look up to his calling! To my friends, it became a normal routine task to respond when my father called for me.

In 1950, when he had a full time job as a joiner, our father kept his promise to the Deaf community to find a venue in Greenock that would be suitable as a meeting place. He came across a lady called Miss White who listened to his challenge and his request for assistance. Miss White became very enthusiastic about the idea and worked hard with assistance from her wide group of professional and influential contacts. Eventually they found a grand mansion in Greenock and established a Board of Trustees, consisting entirely of hearing professionals, to oversee the new 'Hillend Mission for the Deaf'.

In the weeks leading up to the inaugural Opening Day of the Mission, my sister and I were consistently being encouraged by Mother to escort her friends' deaf son David, to his aunt's home in Southgate, London. This involved a journey on the Milk Train and the underground, as he was too young to travel alone. Roba agreed, but I refused to accompany her on a fortnight's holiday in London because I wanted to continue my treasured summer holidays at the seaside.

Roba acted a like a sly fox to find a way to drag me along with her. She asked a friend to act in deception in front of me at the deaf club, by feigning excitement at the thought of being asked to go with Roba and David to London. Roba's scheme worked very well, forcing me to say how unfair it was and then I was trapped into going with them after all!

Despite being tricked by Roba, I am forever thankful for being given that second chance to change my mind and go with them. It turned out to be a wonderful opportunity to explore London, especially as it was also our first visit to England. The trip also became a turning point in Roba's life.

By chance, she was looking at job vacancies in shop window displays in the area around Oxford Circus. She was amazed how many vacancies were related to the fashion industry and spent ages looking at the wonderful shop displays. She immediately decided to try and apply for a job. I remember how Roba instructed David and I to wait in the street outside a shop whilst she went in to enquire further. It was lovely to see her beaming big smile as she came back out into the street and announced that she had been offered her dream job as a dress designer! My first reaction was *Oh, what will Mother say?*

On our return home, Mother was aghast to learn that Roba was to start her job within two weeks. Mother blamed herself for making it happen, but Father was, as always, philosophical. *Never be ashamed to come home if it does not work out well for you.* So, at the age of 21, Roba left home and started a new life in the unknown of London with nobody she could turn to as a friend.

Meanwhile, the Board of Trustees at the Hillend Mission appointed my father as the Superintendent. Fortunately, I was able to watch him at work in the community. To me, he was an amazing man with the ability to cope with the many responsibilities of running the Mission. This new role coincided with a period of convalescence after he had injured his hip joint when he fell from a roof at work. He eventually resigned from his joinery job and focused on his work at the Mission. It became a full-time job, providing a weekly Sunday service, finding suitable employment for Deaf members and other people who were always queuing up at our home, seeking his help to fill in forms. I watched him as he wrote the minutes of meetings, and prepared reports to the Board of Trustees and he also acted as a delegate to the British Deaf Association for three years.

Father ran the Mission with the back up of committees. He also had time to sit with me to share the news of his daily tasks and the outcomes of meetings. One of the many examples that I recall was a wonderful story about a Deaf boy aged 16 who had just left school but was unable to find work, because he was unable to communicate or write due to the poor education he had been given. The boy was living with his widowed mother and he had approached our father for help to find employment. After listening to the boy describe his lifelong desire to work with buses, Father took him along to the bus station and explained the situation to the Manager there. Through perseverance, he managed to persuade them to give the boy a chance and he started work as a floor sweeper. After completing his chores, he would wander around the station, watching the mechanics working on the engines, cleaning and oiling etc. Eventually he persuaded one of the mechanics to let him help with cleaning the engines. As their confidence grew, he was given more specialised jobs and eventually, the bus drivers would not start up their buses until he had given the thumbs up!

As I turned 16, I was forever searching for something to give me more experience in life. I was selected as the Hillend Sports Secretary with responsibility for organising sports matches against both Deaf and hearing teams locally throughout the year. It was a learning curve for me, gaining the right skills, organising events with my father's support. *If you want to be perfect, the only way to learn is from mistakes through experience.*

But unfortunately, things were not as well as they seemed. The Hillend trustees changed the constitution without the consent or knowledge of the deaf members, believing that deaf people should not vote. Father resigned with immediate effect and the following year he was persuaded to start a local independent deaf club. After finding another suitable venue he continued as their secretary/chairman for another six years.

I was becoming aware of my own vulnerabilities in relation to the wider world. Growing up in the MacLean household, communication between my parents, Roba and myself was not a problem as we all used a combination of sign language and finger spelling. I knew there was going to come a time when I would have to leave home and life would be so much different in terms of finding work. Obviously this

14

was going to be in the hearing world and so I was wondering how I was going to succeed at communicating and building relationships with hearing people. This preoccupied me to no end and without any direct help or guidance towards my future career; I was at my wits end about what I should do next. The situation hit home hard, I was realising how difficult it was to get on with hearing people and I was especially worried about coping because of communication barriers. As Helen Keller famously said; *Blind people are cut off from things but deaf people are cut off from people.*

Without really knowing what I needed to do next, and not understanding how to go about arranging job interviews, I made my first independent life-changing decision. I had picked up on the good news that was spreading on the local grapevine of a new modern IBM (International Business Machines) factory/ Head Office that had been built in the Greenock Valley and was soon to be opened. So, on an impulse, I cycled straight there with the hope of getting a job. When I arrived, I could see flags and bunting flying in front of the new building. By sheer coincidence, I had arrived just as the official Opening Day was getting underway! The IBM directors and management were stood outside the main entrance, waiting to welcome VIPs at any moment and as they were looking down the road, everyone saw me arrive on my bicycle! The newly appointed CEO was very sympathetic and asked me to come back the next day for an interview!

I was so pleased to be offered my first job as an assembler in the IBM Electric Typewriter Department and it was good to know that there were also three other deaf people working in other departments. It was nice to be able to communicate with them freely in the canteen during the lunchtimes. After some time, I felt I just wanted to move on to a better job, so I pestered my Auntie Chrissie to give me a chance to attend the evening typing classes that she ran at the Adult Education College. Eventually she gave in to my pestering with the intention of helping me to gain a Clerk Typist certificate! I passed the course and my certificate is, to this day, the only academic / vocational qualification I have to my name.

I was eventually promoted as a Test Typist checking on the machines before they were sent for export. Things had worked out perfectly for me and I was proud to be able to prove that I could do something for myself. In the meantime, I was broadening my social network and making new friends by travelling to stay at Roba's flat in Finchley, North London, for occasional short holidays. I was also attracted to the lifestyle that England had to offer me. So after working at IBM for five years, I felt it was time to move on with a complete change of life, with new experiences and further challenges.

For my 21st birthday present, my parents helped to pay for me to attend the World Federation of the Deaf convention in Wiesbaden, Germany. It broadened my outlook further and on my return home, I made plans immediately. I arranged for a transfer to the IBM head offices in Wigmore Street, London with a job as Clerk Typist in Human Resources. I also persuaded by sister to allow me to move in with her and her husband George in their new home in Surrey.

At the time, this was for me, the most exciting period of my life; I had made all my own arrangements and started a new life in England with support from Roba and George. I don't know how they managed to put up with me for the next two and half years!!

Moving to live in England, I thought it would be inevitable that I would marry an Englishman, but I had assumed wrong. Within three months of arriving, I started to settle down in my new job and met the man of my dreams at a Deaf social club. He was Hamish from the Orkney Isles, Scotland; the first head-boy of Burwood Park School, Surrey, who worked as an Exhibition Designer for the then Greater London Council (GLC). We got married and lived in a rented apartment in Primrose Hill, London, before moving into our own maisonette in Redhill, Surrey. It was so nice to be nearer Roba and George, and it has proven to be impossible to get away from them even up to now, as today we all live opposite each other on the South coast!

My mother remained Father's staunch ally through all his work with the Deaf community. Right up until her death, she organised the social events programme and was popular and well loved by all of the families and friends that knew her. After Mother's death, Father retired to England and lived out his last 14 years wonderfully with Roba, George and their family.

As I looked back over the lives my parents led, I was taken aback when I read Father's statement to the Board of Education and his philosophy of preparing deaf children for the hearing world. I wish that he was still alive with us and I could tell him about the wonderful journey through my life with my family and FYD and how, without fully realizing it, I had been following his philosophy. Looking back as I do now, I can see where my inner strength and determination has come from. And from this I have drawn my desire to succeed and to ensure that young people get the support they need whenever it is needed.

After five years of working at IBM in London, Hamish and I started a family of our own.

2

The Founding of FYD

Taking time out to stay at home and start our new family gave me yet more opportunity to reflect on my evolving life. Living with Hamish and benefitting from our close proximity to George and Roba's young family, meant that there were few communication problems at our home and our social lives within the Deaf community of London and the South East were busy and fulfilled.

We all struck the balance of finding ways to communicate with hearing people at work but not to the extent that we could form any meaningful friendships and extended networks. It was never for a lack of trying on our part as I, like many other deaf people, had been trying to make friends with hearing people for ever and an age, but it was never easy have extended conversations what with a flurry of paper as I tried to write things down and keep things going. All of this was just exhausting and it really wasn't the best way to put others and myself at ease with each other.

When I was seven month's pregnant with our first child Fiona, I learnt of a Christmas fundraising event that was taking place in Redhill. I decided to go and investigate as I saw this as another opportunity to meet new people. It turned out that I struck gold, as it was two teachers of the deaf who were running the event. Denis and Eileen Uttley were trying to raise money for a community project that they had just started for deaf children. I immediately took to them, enjoying their company and the warmth of their friendship with the group of volunteers working with them. I had nothing but admiration for their tireless energy, volunteering all this time and effort on top of their busy professional lives as teachers and so I decided to get involved. I realised very quickly that Denis was a man of great vision, and very industrious, and through all of this, he became a hub that drew deaf and hearing people together.

Denis had been building a successful career as a Merchant Seaman but he had developed a stammer that was making things difficult for him at work. He therefore decided to make a career change and re-trained to become a Teacher of the Deaf. His first job was at the Manchester School for the Deaf before he moved to the Old Kent Road School for the Deaf in south-east London. He believed that his pupils needed the company of hearing children to help widen their language and communication skills and so he began with an evening group after school and organised trips and outings during the weekends and school holidays. At the beginning, the outings were mainly local but after a while, becoming a little more adventurous, they began to explore continental Europe in Denis's trusty van. The children began to get together for weekend activities and then six years later, with grants from their first sponsor, the Allen Lane Foundation, Denis purchased a new minibus.

All this activity was giving deaf and hearing children common experiences and subjects around which they could talk to each other and build lasting friendships. Denis' exceptional attention to detail was all about adapting and designing the environment so that it facilitated ease of communication. Well ahead of his time, he re-arranged the seating in the minibus so that the crew-seating stretched along the length of the vehicle, which meant that the passengers were sat facing each other. This, of course, meant that they could communicate more effectively face to face and everyone could enjoy the same conversation if they so wished.

To cover the cost of petrol, Denis raised money by selling bundles of firewood outside his home in New Malden, Surrey. He sought out mothers who were willing to organise activities to zoos, beaches and other places of interest so that the trips were fun and enjoyable and over time, everyone began to value their growing friendships. By the time I had got involved as a volunteer, Denis had become convinced that his pilot project was successful enough to formally register it as a charity. After much deliberation he decided to call it 'Friends for the Young Deaf' (FYD) and he began to seek out possible deaf and hearing trustees and mothers of deaf children as volunteers. The first meeting of the proposed trustee board took place in 1966 and I was absolutely thrilled. Our little project was really getting somewhere – we were really beginning to make a difference!

Fiona was born with fully functioning hearing and without hesitation; our family doctor recommended that she start full-time Nursery at the age of six months so that she would be able to develop speech and language in a hearing environment. It goes to say this was a difficult time for me as a new mother and I hated being separated from my very young child. Not being able to be part of her early life was the cruelest thing that could happen. Leaving her behind at the nursery every day would leave me in tears – I couldn't understand why I had to do this? It just wouldn't happen today would it? My coping mechanism was FYD; I threw myself into everything I could so that I was busy and the time flew.

In 1967, Denis and the Trustees formally registered FYD as a charity and I was a founder member. My second daughter Morna was born at this time and at six months old, she joined Fiona at the nursery. But despite my involvement with FYD, I was beginning to feel more and more isolated at home and increasingly cut off from the hearing community. It got so bad, that some days I just couldn't wait for Hamish to return home from work, so I could find out from him what was happening in the outside world. I had two hearing daughters and I was desperate to bring hearing people into my circle of friends so that there was balance and perspective. But it wasn't long before help came my way from Diane Kenyon, who was to become a trusted and lifelong friend. Originally from Liverpool and partially deaf, she was to became one of London's top ten catwalk models. She was married to the delightful Andrew who was deaf too.

When we moved to London (1960-1961) Andrew and I decided that it would be a good idea to set up a discussion group with other deaf people. The early group included Andrew and myself, Angela Terry, Alison Heath, Christine Arnold, George and Roba Drewry, possibly George's brother Ralph, Davina Pritchard and others. Christine suggested at one meeting that she bring along a Teacher of the Deaf to meet us as he was doing weekend work with the deaf children in his class, many of whom had additional disabilities. Her guest at that meeting was Denis who talked to us about his work and the reasons why he was doing it. He felt that deaf children needed to broaden their experiences and the world needed to meet them in order to understand what it meant to be deaf. He offered to visit us all separately in our homes and Andrew and I welcomed this.

When Denis came to our home, he told us how he and some hearing parents of the deaf children that he taught had set up a group called FYD, but what he felt was lacking was the input of deaf people. He asked if we would join him and the parents on a residential weekend and we did. We were perturbed to see how little the parents knew about deafness, and even less about deaf adults and how to communicate and socialize with them.

Denis continued to visit our home and a short time afterwards, asked if he could bring along a young teacher who had a deaf daughter. This was Ken Carter, and our friendship with Ken grew into what was in all probability the very first deaf/hearing family link.

Andrew and I organised the first Thorpness Weekend for deaf and hearing families and individuals where deaf and hearing people learnt how to help each other and enable deaf people to reach their potential. Denis brought along professionals and parents of deaf children and we brought along deaf people. In this way, and through Denis and Andrew working on finding funds and grants, they met and introduced David Hyslop and Dawn Jarret, Terry and Ethel Waters, Libby Sheppard and others.

(Diane Kenyon)

Diane knew of my concerns of finding opportunities for my two daughters and so the Kenyon's invited our family to attend our first Easter Weekend in Thorpness. Diane's husband Andrew, an accountant, shared Denis's philosophy of bringing together deaf and hearing adults and their families for the purpose of communication and friendship. Denis helped Andrew to set up the Breakthrough Deaf/Hearing Trust, which was later to be registered as a charity in 1971.

The weekend at Thorpness filled me with great joy as I saw the warmth of friendship and the good communication shown between deaf and hearing families of deaf and hearing children. Everyone appeared to mix well. But what hit me most was when people asked if I could use my voice as well as sign language at the same time. I was momentarily stunned when Dawn Jarret, a partially hearing audiologist and others, said they would like to hear my voice. The thought of using my voice really threw me. Right up to that moment, other people had always told me that I was too deaf to use my voice and benefit from a hearing aid. So I asked Dawn if she would do me a favour and test my hearing. The outcome of this was that I was fitted with a powerful hearing aid and, with this, I could hear. And ever since then, it has always been lovely for me to hear sound around me, especially the voices of our children.

In no time, this new experience encouraged me to use my voice more; starting at first with the children in our families and with the new hearing friends we had made through Breakthrough and FYD. Oh what an experience! I can always remember how my poor sensitive throat became very tender, as I wanted to talk so much! But after a while, the soreness went away and it was great to be able to use both my voice and sign language at the same time, although I knew my speech would never be perfect. It was reassuring to see that when people got to know me better, they are able to tune in to my speech without difficulty. This became a really positive time for me, as the saying goes *Seeing is believing* and I resolved to tell myself that there was no turning back to the old world now, but we would forge ahead and do what we could to help improve the quality of life for other families; to help prepare them for the hearing world.

Working with Denis Uttley was absolutely life changing. The idea of inclusion and integration between deaf and hearing people was powerful enough to drive some to make critical career decisions. Hamish and I met many new friends on our first weekend in Thorpness, and one of them was Ken Carter, who was there with his wife and daughter. He describes his encounter with Denis:

> When I was training to be a Teacher of the Deaf at the Institute of Education, University of London in 1967, I was sent on one of my teaching practices to the Old Kent Road School for the Deaf. It was there, that I was assigned to work with a certain Mr. Uttley. It was before this teaching practice that I was seriously thinking of giving up work with deaf children and returning to the world of sport and academia as I didn't see myself grappling with the complexities of deafness, very low levels of achievement and I was somewhat disillusioned with the university course which I was attending. The very first class I observed was breathtaking and I knew that this man Denis Uttley was going to change my life for ever through his passion for teaching and wanting the very best from his pupils who were not only deaf but had multiple disabilities.
>
> It was whilst I was on this 'aspirational' teaching practice that I went with Denis on his famous London walks with his deaf children learning about Chaucer, Dickens, Shakespeare, Wordsworth and all the people who have

Ken Carter

made a difference, to not only London, but to the rest of the world. It was at this time that FYD was being established that he started taking children down to Romney Marsh in Kent and to places in Europe using his famous FYD vans which were driven by parents and teachers. He wanted to open their minds to the wonder of history and the universe so that they became natural & self –motivated learners.

(Ken Carter)

Out of the blue, Fiona contracted German Measles at the age of two and a half. As a consequence, she became partially deaf. This meant that Morna was now the only hearing person in our immediate family. The positive experience and discovery from the Breakthrough Easter weekend spurred me on to do ever more for my family and I went in search of somebody who could help to develop my speech further. Finding the right advice was a real struggle; but I persisted and eventually, a local health visitor referred me to a retired speech therapist. But she was only able to work with me once a week and then, for only 30 minutes. This was immensely frustrating, as I wanted to spend much more time on my speech, so that it would improve faster. But I was grateful for the help because there was nothing else at that time and something, was better than nothing. One of the key hearing people I met in these early days was Evelyn Carter (Evelyn Stewart as we knew her then).

I remember meeting deaf people for the first time as if it were yesterday.
It was 1969 and I was working as Matron for a self-help group of mothers and their children in London. This had nothing to do with deafness but people who wanted to be in a position to make their own decisions, e.g. to help themselves. Then I met some deaf people who had heard of this concept of self-help groups who also wanted to be in charge of their own lives. They invited me to their New Year's Party in order find out more about their issues and I went along with some trepidation. I thought: Deaf people and a Party? How does that work? You have to remember that this all took place over 40

years ago and the concept of Deaf Awareness had not been created.

Arriving at the home of Roba and George Drewry I pressed the doorbell, as you do, when the porch light started flashing. I panicked. What had I done? Someone opened the door and invited me in, and slowly I began to realise that the flashing lights were a very clever way of letting deaf people know there was somebody ringing their front door bell.

Communication was difficult that night. Everybody was very friendly and chatty, but I found it hard to understand what was being said. So, I smiled and nodded a lot and I am still wondering to this day what I might have agreed to in my ignorance.

It did not get any easier when I tried to speak. Anybody who needs to lip-read would have a thankless task to follow the miss-pronunciations of a foreigner (German in my case) who was not very fluent in English. But, never mind, after food and drink we were treated to some memorable mimed stories by Ian Stewart and other guests which had me in fits of laughter. No language needed here – and such FUN.

On the way home I took stock of the evening and realised that my communication skills with deaf people were very poor but I thought I might be able to help in other ways. I had noticed that some hearing children of deaf parents may not have as much access to activities as their peers and I started to invite them to outings that I organised for my mothers and their children, which seemed to work very well.

With time, I learned a little more about each group and their needs, but when I asked Morag: *What is it like being deaf?* she answered honestly: *I don't really know what it is like being hearing.* This was a light-bulb moment for me and I realised that we needed bridge-workers to fill the gap.

Most of the people I had met that evening were deaf and we had great fun developing opportunities to involve the local community in our integration projects. These would prepare the ground for the next generation of deaf children who should not have to face the same prejudices as their parents and other deaf people. This was mainly the early work of the Breakthrough Trust, once it was established. I remember Diane Kenyon saying: It is important for the deaf adults to reach out and integrate with the hearing community if we want our children to be part of that world, otherwise they may come back to us and say: *But, what have You done to help Them to understand our needs better?*

(Evelyn Carter)

During those first three years of young motherhood, life was an eternal rollercoaster, the highs; times when I absolutely loved nurturing my two small daughters, and the lows; enduring the painful moments of parting when I left them at the nursery. And it was in these moments, when left alone at home with time on my hands, that I worried and fretted about our futures and the potential negative impacts of us being marooned alone, isolated from both deaf and hearing communities. But when I began to look ahead and think about moving things forward, instead of just being a good *stay at home mother*, things began to look up.

I began to develop a dream, that one day everybody, deaf and hearing alike, would be able to communicate with each other without fear of rejection or embarrassment. But the question facing me was how was I going to turn my dream into reality?

I continued to volunteer my time to both the FYD and Breakthrough projects. In 1971, Fiona started school at the Riverview Partially Hearing School and by sheer coincidence, Denis' wife, Eileen, became Fiona's teacher all the way through her primary years, until she won a place at Mary Hare Grammar School.

In 1972, I was invited to become a Trustee of FYD and the following year, I was appointed Chair. What was attracting me to FYD was that it was progressing a unique philosophy which I understood very well and which I have stood by ever since. Quite simply, I didn't want to see any young deaf children go through the problems that I had to endure.

The FYD activities were a mixture of adventure, sports and arts projects that young deaf people enjoyed without their disability imposing any limitations. However, if a young deaf person showed an aptitude for a sport that was not sufficiently catered for in the school curriculum it was extremely difficult to find outlets for this enthusiasm in the community. Sports facilities and coaches were available but communication difficulties prevented young deaf people from accessing and enjoying them. I felt that we needed to re-design our activities to help address these communication problems by providing an environment in which deaf and hearing people could break down communication barriers and enjoy their sports of choice.

This thinking began to sow the seeds for the development of the first major FYD project – the Millfield Summer School in Somerset. Ken Carter was a former a pupil, so, with our new ideas in mind, he got in touch with John Davies the school's Sports Director. Ken asked John if he would consider accommodating an FYD group of six deaf young people with four FYD volunteers, including our family, on the renowned Millfield summer school. John was immensely positive and was happy to give it a go. He proposed a pilot for the following summer as he thought it would be good for the sports coaches to learn how best to engage and communicate with deaf young people in a practical way.

Due to having attended Millfield School on a Sports Scholarship, I was in a good position to discuss with John Davies, the main organiser, the prospect of a group of young deaf people coming to join in with the Millfield Summer School. He fully supported the idea especially if FYD could help with organising the recruitment/ administration including communication facilitators etc. So Morag & I were able to get things going for Residential Integration Courses for young deaf people and their families.

(Ken Carter)

The Millfield project began in 1975 and was an instant success. It ran for the next 18 years and was to change the lives of hundreds. One of the first children to attend was Jane Cole, nee Leaman, who was profoundly deaf and had a younger, partially-hearing sister. They were brought up in a hearing family and although Jane knew a few other deaf children at the PHU[1] she attended, they were integrated into mainstream classrooms for the majority of their time. Jane moved on to the local grammar school and had the assistance of a visiting peripatetic teacher of the deaf. Although her schooling gave her a good command of English, which enabled her to *move reasonably well between both deaf and hearing world,* she had not, at that time, recognised herself in relation to other deaf children. It was just by coincidence that Jane and her sister were at Millfield in 1976, totally unaware of the existence of FYD.

I can remember as though it were yesterday, my first introduction to FYD and the total revelation that there were all these other deaf children out there that were like me! It was also my first introduction to the world of BSL[2] and this strange new language that I'd never seen before fascinated me. I think it was 1976 and my sister and I had been sent to Millfield for a summer sports activity holiday (on the recommendation of hearing friends of my parents), so we had not booked to go with FYD, but when we were there, there were all these children in our groups who were DEAF!! I have no idea now which boarding house we were supposed to be staying in, but after the first night, we never went back there (except to sleep), as the leaders of the FYD project invited us to go back with their kids every night and join in the fun and games with them. Well, that was it; Jo and I were hooked and begged our parents to let us go back to Millfield every year from then on, only this time booking through FYD!

FYD was a HUGE part of my life for years afterwards and I look back very fondly on the friendships that I made (and still have to this day!)

(Jane Cole)

It was a real blessing when I was offered a part-time job with the Breakthrough Trust as their Community Deaf/Hearing Integration Officer in 1977. This enabled me to work from home and it gave me an opportunity to combine practical experiences from both my father's guidance on the values of life, responsibility, reliability and the trust I was developing in people through the philosophy of Breakthrough. I was able to put myself into practical situations where I was working with both deaf and hearing families in partnership with other deaf/hearing co-workers. I also had

---

1   Partially Hearing Unit (PHU)
2   British Sign Language (BSL)

Morag with Denis Uttley, founder of FYD. (FYD)

the staunch support, in every shape or form, from Breakthrough trustees who have since become close friends (Ken Carter, Evelyn Carter and of course, Diane Kenyon). At a later date, another great friendship formed with David Hyslop (Deaf) who was employed as the Director of Breakthrough Trust to work with Andrew Kenyon. We all worked together to offer a range of activities for Deaf and hearing families and this work continues today, under the aegis of DeafPlus.

My job at Breakthrough was about creating opportunities for adults as well as children, but my real affinity and passion was the emerging FYD/Breakthrough interface where our activities were directly supporting deaf and hearing children and young people. I took the lead in developing this joint work further until it emerged as a standalone under the title of *Communication Through Sport* in 1978. A year later, with the blessing and encouragement of the Trustees, I left Breakthrough to take up a full time post as the Director of the FYD Trust and *Communication Through Sport* was the foundation upon which I built the organisation.

Both FYD and Breakthrough were unique because they were both deaf-led, supported by a mix of trustees who were both deaf and hearing. Denis Uttley was a true friend to the deaf and he was really excited to see the growth of FYD under deaf leadership. Ken Carter describes what was motivating Denis at the time:

During the early years of FYD, deaf children were rarely referred to, or even presumed illiterate, as their low standard of reading and writing was often accepted by parents and those professionally involved and put down to deafness. Denis passionately wanted to change this situation for the sake of the next generation. He knew that deaf children were cut off from most of the common communications that provides conversation (chat, over- hearing, small talk, discussions etc.) tapes, records, music, theatre, cinema, telephone and sadly conversation and discussion within the family.

I realised, that through FYD and the early work of Denis and his small army of volunteers, there was a need to involve far more people, deaf and hearing, to provide the background of effective communication and open up opportunities for children and especially for young deaf people to work together on educational-experience type projects and activities. More Friendship and Integration were of paramount importance to create the right environment for tackling age old segregated and 'blinkered' thinking.

(Ken Carter)

As our eldest daughter Fiona was approaching her fifth birthday, Hamish and I became concerned about finding the right information about educating deaf children. We went along to a presentation by Michael Reed hosted at the Royal National Institute for the Deaf (RNID) where we met Jackie Brookes. Jackie is a hearing mother who also has deaf and hearing children and so had been encouraged to go along and meet some deaf adults; this was the beginning of a life long friendship and now we are related through the marriage of our children for whose sake we were attending that meeting:

We had three small children, two deaf and one hearing and until then I knew nothing about deafness and had never come into contact with any deaf people. In those days there were few opportunities for integration.

I wanted our two deaf children to have opportunities and experiences that hearing children took for granted and also for our hearing son to be aware that deafness affected other families too. I guess what I was seeking for the whole family was total integration.

I voiced my concerns to a peripatetic teacher of the deaf who put me in touch with the Rosie family, Morag and Hamish and their two small daughters. Communication was difficult initially, but with a sense of humour and patience we began to understand each other and so developed a long lasting friendship.

(Jackie Brookes)

As FYD's first salaried employee; funded by the Penguin Trust whose support came about as a result Denis's endless letter writing to Penguin founder, Sir Allen Lane, I was at the helm of a ship that was going to realise me my dreams, but, we had only had £200 in the bank! The Trustees gave me free reins to shape FYD on the basis of its aim of providing meaningful *Friendship Insurance* for deaf and hearing children. I was also given the task of controlling administration, fundraising and programming etc. I continued to do this, working from home whilst looking after our daughters and using the third bedroom as my office:

The first I remember of mum starting to build FYD was her setting up office in the small, spare bedroom at home. This was her hub for a long while and meant she could keep her finger on the pulse at home, and dedicate her long working days to creating and building FYD.

(Morna Elliott)

In my attempts to be connected to the real world, I had use of an old, redundant, Post Office tele-printer that could only be used to communicate with others who had similar devices at home or at work. I really needed someone to deal with phone calls on my behalf. Luckily, our next-door neighbour Mrs. Claydon, kindly offered to publish her number on FYD literature so that she would deal with incoming calls on my behalf. This was a most welcome gesture and we strung a 3 amp electric cable between our homes, enabling Mrs. Claydon to press a button by her window that activated flashing lights, to let me know whenever she received incoming calls. I would then pop round to work with her and receive the calls. We also did this for outgoing calls too. It was a working relationship that turned out very well indeed and gave my wonderful neighbour some spice in her life too because she was housebound due to her disability.

With the FYD projects, we were discovering how important it was to provide a controlled environment which allowed deaf people to flourish in an integrated setting where deaf young people were in the majority and hearing were the minority, in order to appreciate what it was like for their peers. As our ideas seemed to work, we developed a strict FYD policy that the participants on each project had to be based on a ratio of three deaf to one hearing (3:1).

We knew then, that integration was a vital and necessary tool to prepare deaf young people for the very competitive hearing world. We also saw this as an opportunity for hearing young people to gain a better understanding of deafness by working in a practical and hands on way. And on top of this, everyone was getting a better understanding of their chosen sport and its associated terminology through the use of interpreters or communicators.

How and where was I going to take FYD to where it needed to be? I was restless and wanted to be sure we were on the right path to achieve our dream. I should have known better, because as I started to feel my way, it all began to happen …

3

The Development of FYD
(1979–1986)

Sharing a plan brings results

In the process of looking where next, what path, how we were going to build things, my prayers were answered. Our daughters were old enough to understand that I didn't want to continue as a stay-at-home working mum and that I needed to find a proper space to work; to be amongst other people during the working day and part of the bustle of the workplace.

When you have a plan, or a need, it's important to share this with others and let them know what you are looking for. It wasn't long before one of our volunteers tipped me off that charity leaders in Sussex held monthly meetings at a place called the East Court Mansions in East Grinstead. In a flash, I turned up at the next available meeting with one of our stalwart volunteers who came along to help with communication.

Good things started to happen almost immediately. First, the Mayor of East Grinstead asked what he could do for us, and so I explained we needed our own base and that I'd now outgrown the home office, it was time to ramp up. He mused over this and said he would call back as he had a room in mind but didn't say where it was. Another gentleman, Christopher Moore, came forward and introduced himself as a solicitor as well as chairman of the local Lions Club. He wanted to know what equipment and office furniture I would need and also offered his valuable legal services if ever we might need them.

Not long after that first meeting, I received great news from the Mayor; he offered me a room in the East Court Mansion, which was owned by the Town Council, free of charge for two years! I was stunned, it was such an amazingly generous offer and when I saw the room for the first time, I just didn't know what to do. It was up on the top floor of the building with magnificent views of the surrounding deer park and countryside upon which the Lord of the Manor used to hunt with his pack of hounds. It was all so hard to take in. I was so overjoyed and couldn't believe my luck.

This was my office! Mine, ours, FYD's office! I was living the dream, which just got better and better as Christopher Moore made good on his promise, and along with other members of the Lions Club, provided the office equipment that I needed

East Court Mansions: FYD Offices 1979 – 2002 (FYD)

to get me going. At first, I began to turn up for work alone at East Court, but shortly afterwards, I was joined by two local volunteers who offered to take turns to come in one day a week to help me with administration and telephone calls. But what's more and to top it all off, my neighbour was happy to look after Morna for an hour each day after school, until I returned home from work. This arrangement suited her because by then, Fiona was away as a boarder at Mary Hare Grammar School.

Reflecting and Discovering

Once we were settled into our office routines, I began to reflect upon what we were learning from the Millfield project. We were just about to start our fifth season and we now had a project that was aimed at encouraging young deaf people to realise their potential through sport, art and other activities, in doing so, broaden their horizons and achieve greater integration with their hearing peers. We understood way back then in 1978, that playing sport developed confidence and we could see for ourselves, how it encouraged young deaf people to work on an equal level with their hearing peers. All of which in turn helped to develop their personalities as well as maintain physical fitness and agility.

Millfield was becoming our flagship and the key driver of the *Communication Through Sport* programme where the development of speech and sign language was a concomitant as it was giving young deaf people the skills and confidence to approach hearing people in other spheres of life; making them aware of deaf people as a constituency and the challenges they faced with communication. Furthermore, how they, as hearing people, could enormously from having deaf friends. We could also see that the development of leadership qualities in young deaf people was going to be vital for the future of deaf/hearing communication and sport was to be the valuable and enjoyable means of achieving this.

We were discovering that Millfield was an important environment for hearing people too. At the end of each Millfield week, the participants were awarded certificates that noted their huge achievements and gave them a big morale boost. When the young people thanked their coaches for all their support coaching and counseling, the coaches returned the compliment, thanking the young people who had helped them develop their own understanding of the communication and linguistic needs of deaf children.

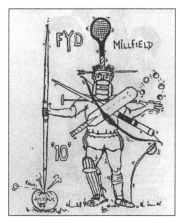

Millfield 1985 (John Wheeler)

Millfield c1978 back row, Alan Brookes and Hamish Rosie with students from their Painting and Drawing classes. (FYD)

In coming together and living on the Millfield campus for a week, the FYD group, including all the communicators and interpreters, had an extended opportunity to get to know each other. Outside the coaching programme, the participants learnt to relax together and enjoy the differing entertainments we laid on. Here there was much laughter and fun as we all enjoyed other's friendship made, of course, ever more special as there were few communication barriers to scale. As is often found with many residential youth projects, there were the usual tears on departure with avowed sworn intentions to return again the following year. Such was the success and pull of Millfield.

For the volunteer communicators and interpreters, the project became very popular as it helped those wishing to enter the profession an opportunity to increase their sign language skills and edge them further to the holy grail of a qualification. It was a blessing that we had qualified interpreters who were prepared to volunteer their time to help others, because, not only were they working – and working very hard – they were there as friends, mixing and socialising with all.

The Millfield Week was now so popular that we had to limit the numbers to 60 participants each time. It was proving to be a near perfect model of integration between deaf and hearing people and I wanted to find a way to replicate it on a national scale, so that many more could benefit from the experience. To share our knowledge and experience, we came up with the idea of running workshops for sports coaches so that we could make their coaching sessions more accessible. We also wanted them to practice what they had experienced on the workshops, by continuing to deliver coaching sessions to deaf and hearing children out in the community at FYD outreach events.

The continuing success of the Millfield Week spoke for itself, and we were able to win major grants from the Sports Council to grow our ideas through FYD Sports

Jackie Brookes, Angela Stanzl, Annie and Clive Rees. Helpers at Millfield. (FYD)

Coaching Seminars and the FYD Sports Festival at Crystal Palace, London.

Our planning for the first seminar had been going well and we were expecting a very good turn out of coaches; three sizable groups of deaf children, accompanied by their teachers and two communicators, had all registered. But then, the day before, lightning struck twice! The first bolt from the blue was a telephone call from Ken Carter apologising that he was unable to attend as a tutor because of a sudden death in the family. Despite this, we still had Chris Lewis our second tutor available, so we thought everything was under control. But then the second strike came, a call from, yes, Chris to say that he had come down with the flu! I had to make a decision – cancel or go to Plan Z! Luckily, Angela Stanzl, another of the volunteers for the day, who was also a Teacher of the Deaf like Ken and Chris, volunteered to take over their duties. She had a lot of homework to do that night; mugging up on the presentations Chris and Ken planned to deliver.

Despite these challenges, the seminar was a great success, masterminded by Angela who worked extremely hard with the support of two sign language teachers, who ran a short course in sports specific signs and associated terminology. Every coach learnt much from the hands-on experience of being able to apply the theory and methodology taught to groups of happy and excited deaf children.

At the end of the day, we hit another high when many of the coaches agreed to support and participate in further FYD projects. This was especially important for us. Two coaches, in particular, stood out from that first seminar; Marlene Swift, a swimming coach, who lived and worked near our offices in East Grinstead and John Lake, a PE tutor at Southwark College, who was to eventually help us to run the first

Crystal Palace Sports Festival 1984 (FYD)

FYD Sports Leaders course a few years later.

Both Marlene and John were instrumental in helping us put together the first ever FYD Sports Festival. For this signature event, we approached Brian Slade, the man in charge of the Crystal Palace Sports Centre, London. Brian immediately liked the idea of a pilot Sports Festival and was good enough to throw in the provision of residential accommodation for anyone who needed to stay overnight. After the usual whirlwind and blur of putting an event together, it was exciting to see our Festival emerge with an array of 60 deaf children, communicators, coaches and parents attend, all backed by Brian and his excellent team. The Crystal Palace management staff worked hard to help us select and programme the differing sports, showing us how to book the various facilities we needed and how to make sure the children were in the right place, at the right time, for the activity they had signed up for!

The concept of the Sports Festival was a new experience for everyone concerned; with each child being able to try out four new sports throughout the day. We needn't have worried, the day went well and Marlene and I came away with a big smile. A representative of the Sports Council was in attendance and it seemed they were pleased with the way their funding was being used. The Crystal Palace Festival was to become our biggest annual event and it grew in scale such that, eventually, attendance numbers at each festival reached their hundreds. In time, we expanded the Festival concept to other areas of the UK including Newcastle, Birmingham and Glasgow.

In the early 1980s we began to plant the seeds of the National Leadership

One of our early activity days at Roba's stables. (Drewry/Rosie family archives)

Training Programme. The Leadership Programme came about because our developing experience with the various activities we were running, told us that we needed volunteers who would be able to put together and run events in a way that reflected our emerging principles and way of working. We required a project management workforce that would be able to develop and disseminate the work programme and the growing FYD brand. From this need we originated a Foundation Leadership course to develop the skillsets of our project volunteers so that they could effectively perform as leaders alongside other professionals such as coaches and teachers. We needed one leader per course and/or activity to ensure that deaf participants were able to get an understanding of the terminology of the sport or other activity being taught.

Our preliminary testing ground for this course was an activity day at my sister's home in Surrey. Once again we had the benefit of Marlene's input as she acted as a coaching model, working in partnership with either a deaf or hearing leader to ensure sporting skills were presented clearly and coherently. Demonstrating our ideas and theories in such a practical way was such fun and we were endlessly amused by the different role-plays we enacted. The first Leadership course went well. We knew from our testing that adults enjoyed this type of learning and it was the same for the young people. They all wanted to go on and qualify as leaders. We were now beginning to see that there was a real need to broaden the knowledge and confidence of young deaf people to prepare them to be both leaders and future professional trainers.

Resourcing and Manpower

By the time we had been at East Grinstead for three years, the growth of the Trust led to what was to be the ongoing dilemma and challenge of core administrative costs versus restricted project costs. We needed funds to sustain running the office and our administrative costs as well as our ever-increasing activities. One day, I was discussing my problems with Roger Sydenham the Chief Executive of the RNID who responded by offering to send two of his staff to meet us at East Court and find out more. The upshot of all this was that the RNID awarded us a two year grant of £10,000 which came just in the nick of time to cover my salary and office rent. It also enabled me to employ Marlene as my full-time administrative secretary in place of our two part-time volunteers. This timely and fantastic support from the RNID helped me to carry on with the development of the organisation whilst our annual grant from Children in Need was used to subsidise both a number of projects and a minibus. I was very fortunate to have Marlene with me who had been brave enough to leave her job as a secretary. No mean undertaking, but I was delighted she was able to come on board full-time.

As the number of projects continued to increase, we took the opportunity to bring in a young unemployed deaf person to work with us. We purposefully wanted someone we could induct and mentor into the FYD way of doing things. In 1983, we chanced upon 18-year-old Geordie, Craig Crowley, who we appointed as our Trainee Youth Leader. Craig had been educated at Cramlington High School in Northumberland and was unemployed and on a Youth Opportunities Training programme when his friend, Grant Richardson, tried to persuade Craig to join him at Millfield.

> Grant had answered an advert from a BBC Holiday programme that mentioned about a deaf-hearing group at Millfield. At first I wasn't keen because £110 was prohibitive back then, but Grant managed to persuade me to go with him. Looking back, it was probably the best £110 I have ever spent!
>
> (Craig Crowley)

Out of curiosity, Craig agreed to go with his friend. As a mainstreamer, it was his first experience of meeting a mixed group of deaf and hearing young people and the deaf / hearing volunteers. He especially recalls the impact of meeting me in my role as a Deaf person directing FYD. Throughout his childhood and teenage years he had never had the opportunity to meet deaf adult role models and his parents were not given the opportunity learn sign language. By the end of his first week with us, Craig made it very clear to me that he wanted to work with deaf people.

It was some time later that Craig wrote to me asking if I could find some sort of way for him to work within a deaf context. I had made some suggestions at Millfield and he had tried his best by approaching people in the public and health sectors and Deaf organisations, but it was futile. Looking back on my own experiences as a deaf teenager, I reminded myself how lucky I had been to be given the chance to experience various opportunities. So it was definitely time for me to do something in return and so I sought funding with which to employ Craig. We received a grant from the Allen Lane Foundation to employ him on a two-year contract from 1982 to '84 and then Hayward Charitable Foundation until 1985. As for accommodation, he stayed at our home until he found a room locally and I would give him a lift to work in our new minibus. Our home took on a new role, providing refuge for a new 'extended family' of young people who were to stay with us, on and off, over the coming years. Morna remembers the first time we took Craig into our home;

> It took a period of adjustment for him and us but he ended up being family, as he is up to this day. I always love seeing him and he's like the big brother I never had.

Now I was no longer the only deaf person at the Head Office. The team now comprised Marlene, Craig, a senior social worker, David Rose, who was on a six months placement as part of his social work training and myself. We all worked together on project applications, fundraising, socials and promotional events. We were a close-knit team supported by an array of professional volunteers who offered their services with finance, legal matters, administration, fundraising and more. The projects continued to enjoy the full support of the schools to which our young deaf people went, their parents, our invaluable local volunteers and our trustees. All this, in turn, led to increasing support from donors, grant giving bodies and yet more and more people participated in the excellent fundraising events put on by the volunteers.

Craig was hungry for the opportunity to increase his knowledge and hands on experience in the management and organisation of projects and so, with my guidance, he was given a chance to prove himself by taking responsibility for some of the local projects around East Grinstead. It was non-stop for him, all he wanted to do was learn and progress. And what was interesting was that his learning complimented mine as I sought to understand the real needs of deaf young people and see how best to stretch them further.

My next move was to seek out the right kind of courses that young people needed in order to qualify as coaches and/or trainers. It was proved that my timing was right on this when, coincidentally, I was asked by one of the young deaf participant's at the next Sports Festival, *why are all the coaches hearing?* My reply to this rather excellent and perceptive question was that the time would soon come when we would have deaf qualified coaches working alongside the hearing coaches!

In 1983, the Thatcher government created a scheme to tackle unemployment by encouraging charities to apply to the Department of Health and Social Security (DHSS) funding programme to set up *Opportunities for Volunteering* (OfV) schemes. Four organisations worked together to bring this scheme into the reach of deaf organisations and they were known as the *Panel of Four*[1]. This was more perfect timing for us, as we needed manpower to run our projects programme but we didn't have the money to pay for it. The scheme allowed us to provide a three–year volunteering placement for young people so that they could gain valuable work experience and develop skills in project management, administration, public relations and fundraising.

We took on a good mixture of unemployed young people, either direct from school as school leavers, or those who had been long-term unemployed. This enabled them to become aware of each other's communication needs and by working together, they gained a better understanding of how to communicate with hearing people, especially amongst the partner organisations with whom FYD was working. I continued to mentor Craig and we encouraged him to share his practical / theoretical experiences and skills with the new workers. We also worked on his leadership and delegation skills so that he could add even more value to our sports/arts and adventure projects.

The first two people we brought on board under the OfV scheme were Caren Metcalfe and Stuart Harrison. They came to us via very different routes. Despite being profoundly deaf, Caren was already an accomplished international Modern Rhythmic gymnast.

> I first met Caren via her friend Robin Sachs at a social function after a Surbiton Deaf Football match – she told me that she was an elite gymnast so we chatted about FYD which obviously met with loads of jealous eyes from my teammates!
>
> (Craig Crowley)

Craig told me about Caren the next time we met at work. Soon afterwards her parents wrote in to ask if there might be any suitable job opportunities for their daughter. Shortly after this, we were able to take her on. But we didn't see much of Caren around the offices as she was always out on projects; utilising her coaching skills and sports knowledge directly with children and young people. Eventually, Caren found full time employment at Crystal Palace National Sports Centre after being spotted working as a coach at our Sports Festival. If that wasn't a success for us, I don't know what was!

My nephew, Hamish, introduced me to Stuart who had been at Mary Hare Grammar School with him. Hamish was concerned that unlike himself and others in their year group, Stuart had not entered higher education or found employment.

---

1   The Panel of Four: Royal National Institute for the Deaf, British Deaf Association, National Deaf Children's Society and the British Association of Heard of Hearing.

Caren Metcalfe coaching at Crystal Palace Sports Festival (FYD)

I met Stuart at the Mary Hare Open Day in 1983 and after learning about of his background and circumstance, I offered him the opportunity to come and join our scheme.

Within a week, Stuart had resigned from his Youth Training Scheme and was ready to move down from his home in Warrington to join us. My sister, Roba, agreed to take him in as a lodger and it seemed to me this would work out well. Craig and I would be able to pick him up on our way in to East Grinstead each morning. With these plans in place, Stuart loaded up his moped onto the train and journeyed south to Euston Station.

> I had never really travelled through London before. My only experience had been taking the tube back and forth between Euston Square and Paddington in all the years that I was at Mary Hare. There I was at Euston once more with my moped and a few possessions. Using some old AA maps belonging to my uncle, I navigated my way through London and out the other side, southbound on the A23 to Redhill.
>
> (Stuart Harrison)

Before I knew it, Stuart duly arrived at my door attired in his helmet, coat and with his trusty moped parked up in the drive. With barely concealed excitement

Hindleap Warren Camping Weekend c1983 (FYD)

Hamish and Morna helped me welcome him into our home for tea before he followed us out to Roba and George's place.

Stuart's recollection is that the first job we gave him was to organise the filing systems (Craig had already painted the cabinets!). I also took him out with me to meetings and presentations. After introducing our audiences to the Trust, I would ask Stuart to stand up and tell his story. Stuart worked hard in supporting Craig with the planning and preparation of various projects.

The first project we encouraged him to take the lead on was the Hindleap Warren Camping Weekend. Stuart was most confident about this weekend and he worked well with Nick Brookes, an FYD participant and the eldest son of our friends Jackie and Alan. Nick was volunteering during a summer break from Durham University. Both Stuart and Nick had been Scout leaders at school and they were well suited to the rigours of an outdoor pursuits weekend. They competently supported the project volunteers and were excellent and positive role models for the children. Stuart was evidently at home in that environment and made it clear he wanted to do more. Over the next three years he did just that, masterminding a number of very successful projects in partnership with myself, Craig and Marlene.

By 1984, the number of young people coming into the OfV scheme had grown. Malcolm Sinclair, a qualified electronics engineer but working in a road-builders gang, was one. He first volunteered at the Crystal Palace Festival and then went on to earn some coaching qualifications, which enabled him to coach badminton back home in Scotland. Our two families, the Sinclair's and the McGilp's (on my mother's side) were well known to each other. Looking for a career change, he applied to join the scheme:

> Although I had qualified in electrical engineering, job prospects were limited so I applied to work on the Opportunities for Volunteering scheme. This was the start of my professional experience that led me to become a qualified Teacher of the Deaf. One of my very first tasks was to make a cup of tea for Morag. She complained that she liked to have the milk in the cup first, so I went away and made another!
>
> (Malcolm Sinclair)

The 1980s were very exciting times for FYD. With our additional manpower, we were able to attract an ever-increasing number of volunteers to support the growing portfolio of projects and fundraising activities. But what is more, our young people began to get involved in strategic decision-making and the origination of new projects with their own ideas and suggestions. This was definitely ahead of the times and demonstrated that our investment in developing confidence, leadership and decision-making skills was working. Our placement volunteers started to draw in more and more young deaf and hearing people to FYD; all of whom had a desire to enjoy the same opportunities for themselves. We would send our young people out in pairs, initially with a mentor, to promote the organisation at events and other places where young deaf people congregated. Presentations were made in schools, colleges and in the community. After a while, we allowed some to work alone:

> I did not really learn to use sign language until I was about 21. I had been sent by FYD to man a display stand at the City Lit Centre for the Deaf in London. I was there alone, for the entire day, handing out information and answering questions about our work. It soon became apparent to me that I was having difficulty in communicating with young deaf people who used BSL but had minimal English skills and this started to become frustrating for them and myself. So, on the train journey back to Redhill, I got out the BSL alphabet card and made sure that I knew all the signs off by heart and sat there fingerspelling everything I could see around me in a kind of I-Spy game.
>
> (Stuart Harrison)

The enormous benefits of the Opportunities for Volunteering to FYD and, ultimately young people, was eloquently summed up by the RNID in our 1986 newsletter:

> Opportunities for Volunteering offers places each year for young deaf volunteers to work at the communications centre HQ in East Grinstead, during which time they learn basic office procedure and administrative skills and how

to apply practically what they have leant on their leadership courses. Each volunteer is given a series of FYD projects to organise during the year and is responsible for seeing them through from the planning stage to completion. They all respond well to the challenge of responsibility and the opportunities to prove themselves to others and there is a circular effect in that when they have succeeded once they will have the confidence to try more-ambitious ideas. There is also a 'wheels within wheels' effect in that a successful project means that those participating in the project will also have benefitted.[2]

(RNID 1986)

Structuring the Leadership Training

After Craig had been with us for a while and once we had started the *Opportunities for Volunteering* work, we began to seek out formalised training opportunities that would enable young people to qualify as sports coaches and/or trainers. We had our Foundation Leadership Training, which was running well and at first, Angela Stanzl and myself ran the courses in 1981 -82, but then eventually Craig took over with support from Graham Groves a teacher of the Deaf from Mill Hall Oral School for the Deaf. After some research, we came across the Industrial Society Leadership Training Programme and the CCPR Sports Leaders Award. Here was what I was looking for – the means to formalise the content of our Leadership Training.

In the course of her own management training, Evelyn Carter had attended courses delivered by the Industrial Society[3] and saw that they could possibly add value to FYD. Evelyn introduced me to Bob Kent, a Senior Advisor at the Industrial Society and explained our needs. After Bob's colleague, Jerome Ripp (Voluntary Organisations Campaign Leader), had come along to observe our Foundation training, we learnt that we needed a new and bespoke leadership pathway that trained people to become supervisors of teams on our projects. With Bob's help, we piloted a supervisory leadership course that was tutored by Bob and Jerome at the Industrial Society's training rooms in Pall Mall.

The course proved to be an outstanding success as it increased young people's knowledge of the theoretical and practical aspects of leadership. As a result, the participants felt confident about taking on more responsibility and acting as supervisors on our projects. Bob himself continued to deliver these courses and they proved to be very popular with everyone who attended. We now had a training curriculum emerging of action-centred leadership which comprised Stage 1 Foundation, Stage 2 Supervising, which ran for the best part of two years.

We decided to let Craig co-work with Stuart Harrison, under the mentorship of Bob Kent to deliver Stage 1 until we were confident to hand the full responsibility for training over to Craig. To him, it was a big step forward, but I knew from the start that he had leadership potential. Yet it was for Craig to prove himself and he rose to

---

2   RNID Soundbarrier March 1986 The Way Forward: Integration and the FYD
3   Now known as The Work Foundation

Industrial Society Training Weekend, Pall Mall. October 1984 (FYD)

the challenge well, working as Group Youth Leader and a model to both deaf and hearing young people.

I cannot recall exactly how the Community Sports Leaders Award (CSLA) first came to FYD, but we were fortunate to have the support of the GLC/ILEA. When we first approached them to support our work, we were introduced to Kathleen Francis who was their Specialist Youth Officer (Disability). She worked in this role for five years and through her vast contacts in London, we became aware of opportunities, organisations and individuals that would suit and complement our work.

When we approached Nigel Hook at the Central Council of Physical Recreation (CCPR) in 1984, he was very excited at the prospect of working with FYD and was keen to see the course that he had a hand in designing, to become inclusive for disabled young people. From these beginnings, Nigel stayed a very good friend of FYD and Evelyn, Craig, Stuart and I, were always sure of his welcome and support when we made our regular FYD attendances at CCPR Special Interests group meetings. Sadly, Nigel died suddenly in 2006, but his legacy continues to drive the Leaders Award that is now with Sports Leaders UK.

Back in 1984, this course was a big step forward for those who wished to become leaders of our projects. With Nigel's support we also wanted to use the course to create a wider awareness of the communication needs between the CCPR trainer and deaf and hearing participants. Senior Physical Training Instructor Derek Waters led our first weekend at Hendon Police Training College tutoring 26 participants and 8 police cadets. With Kathleen's influence, the Right Honorable Illtyd Harrington, Chair of the GLC came to visit the project and address the group.

The elected members of the Inner London Education Authority liked to see what was going on within the Authority. FYD offered open house to all their events. After a short discussion with Dot Bigwood, Chair of the ILEA, I was instructed to arrange transport and accompany one or two members to the event of their choosing. It was always interesting and visits went well. In Committee, the members described the work of FYD with enthusiasm. Morag obtained what she needed for the FYD programme.

(Kathleen Francis)

Craig Crowley, tutoring at Dukes Barn (FYD)

Unlike the rest of our leadership training, the Sports Leaders Award was accredited by the CCPR and the participants had to complete 10 hours of community sports leadership afterwards. One of those participants looking for a ten hour placement on the course in February 1986 was Clare Ingle, who had initially only entered the award because she was fed up with the snow and icy roads that were preventing her from jogging and attending aerobics.

Clare went to speak to Pauline Rhodes, who was chair of a local NDCS parents group in Bedfordshire, to see if she could suggest some volunteering opportunities with deaf people. Pauline set up a meeting with the head of PE at a girl's high school that had a PHU. The voluntary work involved taking a class of girls for athletics and assisting with tennis. There were no deaf girls in the group, but this didn't matter as they *communicated through sport* and everything was highly demonstrative. Initially Clare had been nervous about taking on a class of hearing girls but she enjoyed it and drew much satisfaction and confidence from it. After completing the requisite 10 hours and gaining her award, Clare went on to supervise a deaf children's' play scheme during the summer holidays. She also started on a FTEC (FE Teachers certificate) and worked with deaf students at the Barnfield College deaf unit.

Since doing the CSLA course, one thing has led to another for me. If I had not done the course, I would not have met other deaf people in Bedfordshire and would not have had the fun.

(Clare Ingle.)

CCPR Community Sports Leaders Award, Hendon (FYD)

Fond memories of leaders Craig Crowley, John Lewis, Malcolm Sinclair who paid visits to our Norfolk House College regularly and we were smitten by Craig Crowley. One of the events we attended was the gruelling fitness weekend at Hendon Police College and I lost my hearing aid in the snow. Stuart Harrison helped me to find it. That was 30 years ago.

(Lizzie Green)

In 1987 we switched the Sports Leader Award course venue to the Dartford Annex of the London Polytechnic. We did this for two reasons. Firstly, we needed a weeklong course to make it more successful for the delegates who required more time to complete the external tasks that would not have been available at Hendon. Secondly, we wanted to use our own instructor; John Lake, Head of PE at Southwark College, whose expertise and ability to communicate with deaf people was important. Whilst he was at teacher training college, Stuart Harrison, had continued to work on our *Communication Through Sport* programme and with John as his mentor, he went on for Tutor training with the CCPR and delivered our 1987 version of the Sports Leaders Award in Birmingham. All of this was ably supported by the hard work of Chris Ratcliffe (on the *Opportunities for Volunteering* scheme) as one of the first things they all did to make the training accessible, was to gain a special dispensation from the CCPR to extend the course to four days, in order to incorporate some of the post-course activities (first-aid training and some

Chris Ratcliffe (second left) and others CCPR Sports Leaders, Bexley, Kent. (FYD)

supervised practical coaching) that were difficult to arrange for deaf students as they needed communication support. This enabled deaf participants to complete the certificates with the minimum of delay.

Communication Through Sport

In the meantime, our *Communication Through Sports* programme was beginning to attract a wide range of playing standards participants and so our emphasis was focused on providing quality coaching for all. Sue Pegler, an LTA tennis coach, had joined us in 1982 for the Millfield week and the good standard of play, encouraged her to work with us to organise the first tennis weekend for about 15 players. The fee of £25 was a large sum for families to pay for an introductory course and we were finding it difficult to fill the available places, as many families had not yet realised the added value and significance of our work, not only for the coaching opportunities, but also for the social development benefits as well.

Naturally, the course was popular with the more advanced players and so we concentrated on those who had aspirations to compete internationally by running advanced coaching weekends at Bisham Abbey, where sponsorship enabled us to keep the costs at a reasonable level. Sue also arranged a number of coaching competitions in France with her coaching colleagues in Europe, so that our more promising players could enjoy their first taste of international sport.

On Sue Pegler's insistence, we arranged for Craig and Marlene to train for the Tennis Teachers certificate run by Dudley Georgeson, one of the foremost thinkers of tennis. I was delighted to hear that with Marlene's support as a communicator, Craig passed his examinations with flying colours and became our first Deaf Tennis Teacher. This proved one of my points that deaf people needed support and guidance on these types of courses and set precedence for the future pathway for deaf people in sports coaching.

The 1985, we organised the Bisham Abbey weekend with guidance from Sue and coaching from Dudley and his assistant Tati Hurd. The weekend was completed with trials to select players for the trip to France. It has to be said, the French trip was an eye-opener for all as they discovered that standards of play were much higher in France. Over the next few exchanges, the French began to field weaker teams to compete against our players, in order to give them a more positive experience. My daughter Fiona, had her own suggestions:

'I feel that standards could be improved if a team could be selected (from the trials) at Bisham Abbey to play in a series of matches against strong players of similar ages in local tennis clubs which would do much to improve the match play experience of the team.

(FYD newsletter 1986)

We continued to work in partnership with the Lawn Tennis Association and British Deaf Tennis to provide coaching sessions, weekends etc. On one occasion, we all worked jointly with the RNID through sponsorship from Seiko Ltd to organise a Tennis Day at Bishops Park, Putney. There was tennis coaching for children and a competition for others. There were also plenty of sideshow attractions and celebrity visitors to entertain everyone. Angela Charles-Edwards and William Clapham won their respective events and were rewarded with Seiko watches as prizes. Other winners were Judy Hennessy and David Bassett (Mixed doubles); Gordon Mitchell and Richard Weinbaum (Mens doubles). Cathy Davies and Michael Trimm were winners of the under 18's singles.

By now we had started to organise other sports festivals outside of London and from 1984 onwards, funding and support for the Birmingham festivals came from the Department of Recreation and Community Service in Birmingham and from the staff of Small Heath Leisure Centre. There were about 60 children attending from the local area and from afar as Nottingham and Leicester. Sue Bright described the children's enthusiasm as 'catching' which was evident in the response she received when visiting one of the local schools afterwards – the children recognised her as the 'sports lady' and went on to share their experiences with classmates who had not yet been able to attend.

This was as clear an indication as ever that our work with sports festivals

Bisham Abbey also hosted squash weekends (John Wheeler)

was going to grow. In the West Country, Ann Robinson worked with a team of volunteers who fundraised with a 13-mile sponsored walk and worked with the South-West Region Sports Council to host the Poole Sports Festival. Amongst the coaches attending, was Caren Metcalfe who led a fitness class for parents and their children at the end of the day.

Arts projects – because there is more to life than Sport!

We organised projects to cater for a wide range of interests amongst young people. By 1985 we were hosting our 4th annual painting competition; attracting 250 entries from schools across London and the South East. Prizes were awarded by Lady Anerley, and judged by Lorna Binns, Arthur Hackney William Bowyer and my husband Hamish. TV personality and artist Tony Hart was involved and he was most generous with his support. We were also appreciative of the support shown by TV presenter Floella Benjamin, who often found time to support as many of our activities as she could and who then honoured us by agreeing to be a patron of FYD.

Daphne Payne of the National Youth Theatre of the Deaf explained the real value of the Drama weekends that we provided:

> The real value of these weekends I feel lies much deeper than the little exhibitions of amateur dramatics, although it is always the high spot. For many of the children taking part, it may be their first experience of doing

something creative for themselves. Relatively few children are fortunate enough to be chosen for the 'school play' fewer still ever acquire the highly specialised techniques that make good mime, but anyone can 'do' drama as this weekend showed. Nor must we forget the social aspect – the benefit of bringing children from very different educational environments together for a couple of days, just to 'have fun, to communicate with each other, to exchange ideas and, on the last day, addresses. How many I wonder will keep that promise to 'keeping touch' until we meet again – next time?

(D Payne 1986, FYD Signpost Newsletter)

1985 United Nations International Year of Youth

With support from the GLC/ILEA Youth Team through Kathleen Francis and the Disability Resources team where sign language interpreter, Linda Richards was their Communications Officer, we celebrated the International Year of Youth by hosting a conference for young people. We were able to employ Penny Gunn (nee Saunders-Davies) (Deaf) and Kenneth Wycherley (Hearing) for three months to plan and co-ordinate this headlining event.

Tony Hart and one of the Art Competition winners (FYD)

47

Floella Benjamin keeping everyone enthralled at an Art Competition. (FYD)

I was made redundant from my job as a pastry chef at one of the well known pastry companies. It turned out that it was the right time to apply to work for three months as the project coordinator after my past experiences with FYD as a volunteer and attending a few FYD leadership courses so I went for it. Ken and I worked equally to organise and invite people to attend the conference that took place in the City Hall of the Greater London Council. We formed a committee and called it the Deaf Young Action Group (DYAG), working with Craig Crowley who was chairman. The committee came up with ideas and themes for the event and we settled on *Where are the Opportunities*? and invited a number of young deaf people aged between 18 and 25 years old to come and speak about opportunities in employment and further/higher education.

Also it was amazing how Ken and I managed to communicate well with each other and travelled together to Deaf clubs, schools and other places in London and the South East to promote our event. It was such a great success to see over 300 people turning up and find out what opportunities were on offer. I was very proud to have taken on that role and to be amongst a group of role models showing others what we could do and encouraging others to follow our example.

(Penny Gunn)

One outstanding memory I have of our preparations for the event; I remember us all having a DYAG meeting at David Ingham's parent's home in Surrey. We were waiting for Penny to arrive, to start the meeting. It was also at this time that she was training to run the London Marathon and that morning she had run from her home in Crystal Palace – all the way to Esher as a training run!

(Stuart Harrison)

The conference was held over two days on the 29/30th November 1985. The first day was an open exhibition of over 30 organisations connected with deafness and opportunities for young people and activities associated with FYD. This type of event was very rare in those days and so attracted large numbers. The following day was attended by some 326 delegates who listened to twelve speakers[4] introduced by Edna Mathieson, Vice Chair of the Higher Education Sub-committee, ILEA. The topics covered were Communication, Community, Education, Employment, Politics, Technology, Opportunities and Leadership.

The day ended with a drama performance and a celebratory party on the Thames. I know that this event was of benefit to many young people. It was their contribution to the International year of Youth and the event encouraged both deaf and hearing to strive for more PARTICIPATION and DEVELOPMENT for young deaf, partially hearing and hearing people; to create OPPORTUNITIES and gain a better understanding of their needs and rights within civil society.

Everyone we recruited through the Opportunities for Volunteering scheme was free to leave at anytime if they found a job, or wanted to move on to further or higher education. Some did find work and left, but later returned to us, as their jobs didn't meet their expectations. We tailored their placements as much as we could according to their interests, and also allowed each one of them to take part in overseas experiences with other youth organisations.

Some of the first people to take up these opportunities were:

- Camp America (Craig Crowley, Nick Brookes),
- Journey of a Lifetime (JOLT) (Shirley Thompson); China, Russia, Mongolia
- British Schools Exploring Society; expedition to SE Iceland (Stuart Harrison, Malcolm Sinclair)

At the end of the summer in 1985, Craig had moved on to study at Bulmershe College, Reading. On top of his college work, he continued with the running of leadership training weekends, but his free time was limited, as obviously he had to compete his studies. Fortunately, we were blessed to have Damian Barry on hand who was, by then, ready to take Craig's place as the leader of the FYD Leadership

---

4   Ben Amirpanahi, Jill Coates, Vivian Coward, Craig Crowley, Stuart Harrison, Chris Hurren, David Ingham, Patricia Kiff, Charlotte Moulton-Thomas, Caroline Parker, Chris Ratcliffe, Penny Saunders Davies and Malcolm Sinclair.

Young audience at the DYAG Conference 1985 (FYD)

Deaf Youth Action Group 1985 (FYD)

Training. Damian had worked closely with Craig and was another go-getter, immensely rich in charisma and personality!

It was at this time that Craig was voted President of his Student Union for the second year running by yet another landslide election. I was hugely proud of this and even more so when he went on to give his first public address to 2,000 delegates at the NUS Conference in Blackpool. This landmark occasion enabled Craig to highlight the importance of Deaf students rights in Higher Education. Reflecting on his achievement, Craig recalls how the DYAG conference encouraged him to start thinking in political terms as he realised how limited deaf people's awareness of political matters was. His youth work training now introduced him to the politics of race, sexism, equal opportunity and disability. As President of the Students Union at Bulmershe he launched the National Network of Deaf Students with three clear and strategic aims; to improve the status of deaf students and the range of opportunities open to them; to obtain a better representation of Deaf students in Student Unions and other affiliated organisations and to promote the rights, needs and interests of Deaf students in further, higher and continuing education.

In September 1985, we opened a regional office in London, under the responsibility of Evelyn and staffed by Charles Herd, Development Officer and Karen McArthur as assistant. After an initial period of orientation at East Grinstead, Charles and Karen moved into their London base, awaiting feedback on the DYAG conference so that they could ascertain the real needs of young deaf and explore what areas they should focus their time and energies for development. Meetings were held with many organisations like the British Sports Association for the Disabled and London Youth Games, to try and see where young deaf people could participate.

In the last 8 months new developments have been made with so many enquiries coming in the office is kept continuously busy. A drop-in has been set up and numerous volunteers have come forward offering their services. Other youth projects want to link with FYD. The London Office is a great success. FYD wants to see a strong representation in each of the London Boroughs – to be able to provide services to the local community.

(Cathy Davies interview with Evelyn in 1987)

Whilst the London office became a focus point for the development of projects in London and Home Counties, our teams at East Court were answering an increasing number of requests to set up projects in other areas. But as with everything, this all depended on the funding and resources available.

Following a meeting I had back in May 1985, during our second Birmingham Sports Festival, I met with a deaf man called Martin Beech who with a few others was interested in helping us to open a new group in the Midlands. We agreed to

'Our aims are to promote opportunities and encourage both deaf and hearing children and young adults to engage in sports and creative activities.'
(Martin Beech, centre of photo behind Morag. FYD newsletter, April 1986)

explore this and on the 16th November, met to discuss the idea further and check out their commitment. The meeting was held at the home of Sue Bright and it was there that with formally established the FYD Midlands group with Martin as Chair, Sue as Secretary and John Langard as Treasurer.

1985 was also the year that Denis Uttley wrote to me with his considered reflections on how far FYD had progressed to that point. He was a true and expanse friend to deaf people who, in return, appreciated his warmth and his approach. He was both excited and overjoyed to see the growth of FYD trust under deaf leadership. It inspired him to ask and seek answers for three key questions:

What was special about FYD?

The core philosophy is a work in progress and is ongoing; to search deliberately for what might be termed 'friendship insurance' FOR deaf children (especially those of poor speech) Note the significance, therefore, of the title – Friends FOR the Young Deaf (NOT OF the Young Deaf).

There are estimated eight million people in Britain whose hearing is to a greater of lesser extent defective. There are almost NO direct attempts being made deliberately to find friends for children in this group. Must it always be an area of work just left to chance?

Why was FYD formed?

The present educational system for deaf children cannot possibly provide enough engagement with the vast hearing world in which they are to live their lives. The intensely specialised nature of schooling for the deaf leaves almost no time for deaf children to acquire life-skills through socialisation and mutual learning with OTHER

Denis Uttley tending to the Tree (John Wheeler)

(in their case HEARING) children.

What are Children's real needs?

All Children need fresh air, exercise, green grass, challenges, love and encouragement. Deaf children as well – so how do we give them the same?

> Sow the seeds, you might never see the blossoming, but that is not your concern.
>
> (Dennis Uttley)

4

"Go to Hell!"

I look back with pride on 1986, our seventh year at East Court and we were achieving much on a low budget; dealing with a vast array of 36 different projects. The continued support and feedback from volunteers and participants indicated that we were being successful and helped to inform our thinking as to how we might progress the organisation.

> "We must not take this success for granted however as it is only brought about by the dedication and hard work of many volunteers and FYD staff. The contribution made to FYD's work by volunteers who assist under the DHSS scheme cannot be overstated; they are shining examples of the successful operation of a government backed scheme.
>
> Our success and growth in recent years has been achieved in spite of a constant battle for financial resources. Unfortunately, the future does not appear to be any brighter in this respect and will not be helped by the demise of the GLC who have been great supporters of our work in recent years and of which they are greatly thanked.
>
> I think that the FYD aim for 1986 should be to provide opportunities for more and more deaf children and young people so that they can integrate successfully into the hearing world"
>
> (FYD Chairman, FYD Newsletter April 1986)

Things seemed exciting for everyone concerned. We were all working hard together, but within a few months; I was stunned to find myself locked in an unexpected challenge from the Trustees. One that saw me fighting for my very survival and that of FYD as I knew it.

When faced with the task of looking for new Trustees to replace those who had left, I was usually looking for people whom I could trust and who would bring the right kind of support that we needed to take FYD forwards. In the early years, I learnt that some of the people we appointed never really delivered. I learnt the hard way, not to make assumptions and to try and be clear about our expectations. One example was a reputable businessman from Sussex who was introduced to me through one of our volunteers. He was the chairman of a number of companies and held directorships of others. I had hoped that he would assist me by raising money for our core costs through his network. However, he saw things differently, and I had to respect his view that he believed the responsibility for bringing in funding rested with me.

On another occasion, when it was time to find a new Chairperson, I approached someone who had come to FYD as a volunteer sports coach. He was also someone with judiciary and management experience. Over time, I got to know him and I decided that he was the right person to be the next Chair of the FYD Trust. He was happy to accept my invitation and in the beginning he turned out to be a great asset and supported me in numerous ways. In 1986, he was Chair of our Board that comprised of two hearing trustees (Evelyn Carter and himself) and two deaf trustees.

But things came to a head between the Chairman and myself, as he became ever more dictatorial and kept instructing me as to how I should deal with operational matters. Our relationship started to deteriorate further after I had employed a new administrative secretary at Head Office. The previous three secretaries had been enthusiastic and earnest, helping me with telephone calls and acting as communicators, relaying what was being said between myself and whoever was on the other end of the phone line.

Things started to become difficult when I realised that the Chairman was complaining on the phone to my new secretary, telling her to pass on directions for my attention about some operational matters he didn't agree with. I felt that he was over stepping the mark and that he shouldn't treat me as a subordinate.

And so it came to head. On one particular phone call, I finally had enough of his continued pestering.

June 1986

The Chairman telephoned me at home and my youngest daughter Morna, had to help with the call. At the time, I was angry that he had contacted me at home and felt that he should have held back until I was back in the office or we had met face to face. To have a child relay a call of this type was unacceptable.

During the call, I told Morna to tell him: "Go to Hell".

She refused to pass on my comment, but after I insisted for the third time, she finally passed on the message; 'Morag says, "Go to Hell"'.

Coincidentally, I was due to have a meeting with my secretary to review her job description and the issue of relaying phone-calls was to be a main agenda item. But shortly before the meeting was due to take place, she handed me a memo stating that she wanted her job description to be clarified and reviewed at a forthcoming Trustees meeting.

11th June 1986

The meeting with the secretary went ahead as planned. The first item was the task of taking telephone calls and messages. I tried to make it as clear to her as I possibly could, that this was an important task for me as Director of the charity and I needed this to be done in an objective and positive way. I was about to go through the rest of the items when she stopped me and said that she was not prepared to proceed further. I explained that it was important to go through all the items. She refused to proceed and discuss the matter and before I knew what was happening we were arguing. You couldn't make it up.

I stopped the meeting and gave her time to think things over whilst I went to another room to take part in a recruitment interview. On my return, I discovered that she had left the office. She had not left a note for me (which was unusual) and so I presumed that she needed time to think about the job and where we were going with all of this. At this stage, I had no idea if she was going to come back into work.

13th June

My secretary telephoned the office, saying that she was returning to work the following Monday. She knew that I would be away, attending the BDA Triennial Congress in Rothesay, Scotland for a week.

24th June

My secretary was not in the office on my return to work after the Congress. She had left a note explaining that she had decided to take a week off. There was no indication of her plans to leave the Centre. I sensed something fishy was going on. And it just happened that I was due to see the Chairman the next day at his offices.

25th June

The meeting with the Chairman was previously booked to discuss the Senior Development Officer post for the London area. But at the outset, he put this agenda issue aside and chose to plough on with my secretary's apparent complaint.

I discovered that she had telephoned the Chairman and told him everything that had happened. I told the Chairman that I was not happy with the way he was handling things, because he had not forewarned about his plans to discuss this issue and that he had not allowed me to prepare. I also felt my secretary had been wrong to by-pass me as her line-manager and to go straight to the Chairman. They had both kept me completely in the dark.

The Chairman asked me if I felt the secretary was a competent worker. I replied by saying 'in some areas' but he insisted on my answer being either 'incompetent or competent' so I replied 'incompetent'. He went on to say that the Board of Trustees, with the exception of Evelyn, felt that I was responsible for the breakdown in relations with the secretary.

26th June
I wrote a letter to all of the Trustees to give my side of the situation about what had happened between the secretary and myself.

1st July
The Chairman telephoned the FYD Centre and informed me that my secretary had sent him her letter of resignation. Again, she had not discussed anything with me and communicated directly with the Chairman instead.

4th July –Trustees' Meeting
I understood from Evelyn that at this Trustees meeting, the Chair decided that it was necessary for the Trustees to discuss what had happened between my secretary and myself at FYD Centre on 11th June. He mentioned that he had discussions with both the Trustees Minutes Secretary – and my secretary after his meeting with me on the 25th June.

The trustee's discussions weighed up past criticisms made by the previous Administrative Secretaries of FYD operations / administrations and this new case in question. They, with the exception of Evelyn, felt that I was responsible for this entire happening. The three Trustees agreed that my criticism of my secretary had been unfair and the Chair was more than satisfied with her competence.

Evelyn insisted that she was in favour of giving me a chance to account for my actions in more detail and that the situation should be resolved in a constructive and positive way. She acknowledged the likelihood of faults on all sides, but that I should be given the chance to attend a management re-training course if necessary. The course of action should be to issue me with a disciplinary warning, not dismissal.

The other Trustees decided not to accept Evelyn's proposed course of action, because it was clear to them that my secretary and I could no longer work together and they did not wish to see the secretary to leave. They took a view that *"for the benefit of the Trust and young people it served if the Director was to leave"*.

Evelyn disagreed strongly with this proposal and suggested that if there was any course to follow then they should follow the guidelines laid down by the Employment Protection Act. To emphasize her position, Evelyn threatened to resign if they proceeded with their plan.

Evelyn walked out of the meeting.

I was called in to face the Trustees and the Chairman explained to me that they had held a lengthy discussion and Evelyn had threatened to resign. The others made it clear that they had lost confidence in me and had decided not to renew my contract from 10th October 1986. This was without any oral or written warning, or any discussion and willingness to try and sort out the difficulties between my secretary and myself.

On my way out of the room, I was in an obvious state of shock. Evelyn was waiting for me in a nearby pub to assure me of her support.

5th July

Without wasting time and at 2.00am in the morning, Ken and Evelyn drove to our home… The fight back began. Ken suggested that I should get to Head Office as early as possible to hold my desk whilst grabbing legal advice. The town clerk at East Court Mansions was ordered to change the locks. During the course of the day, I was given two different pieces of advice, one from Christopher Moore, our long-standing and faithful solicitor and the other, from a QC specializing in Charities. Christopher advised me to leave my desk and papers behind. In stark contrast, the QC turned up at my office and went through my contract in the presence of Ken and Evelyn. He advised me to hold my desk whilst we got things sorted. I decided to take the QCs advice as it allowed me to maintain the running of the organisation whilst dealing with legal matters concerning my contract. As well as being a local solicitor, Christopher was a very good friend of FYD and he offered his services pro bono, agreeing to stand behind the QCs advice. He offered to *"be there"* whenever I needed his guidance.

I was now in the hands of Christopher, and I wrote a letter to organisations and individuals who were working with FYD to inform them of the challenges we were facing. As news got out, there was uproar from volunteers and organisations I had worked with over the past 14 years. Offers of support came pouring into the Head Office with people asking what they could do to assist matters.

This was a new experience to me, getting embroiled in legal matters was a first for me and to this day, I am so deeply grateful to volunteers, sponsors, companies and charities such as the NVCO, PHAB, RNID[1] that drew together on my behalf. In addition, Ken, Evelyn, members of the Deaf Youth Action Group (DYAG) and Kathleen Francis. It was such a morally uplifting time, knowing that I had all their support. The DYAG, chaired by Craig Crowley, set up an emergency meeting in London, to allow people to respond to my letter of concern.

6th September
Emergency meeting of DYAG, FYD volunteers and supporters.

The level of outrage at the trustees was immense. The DYAG received 48 replies to their 50 letters of invitation to the emergency meeting. This was an excellent response, especially given that this was before the days of email and social media. There were 13 apologies for absence, which included the three FYD Trustees.

The purpose of the meeting was to give the volunteers as many facts as possible as to why the Trustees had apparently lost confidence in me. As chair of the meeting, Craig, invited all those present to ask relevant questions or seek clarification as to what was happening. He also explained that following the meeting, all their

---

1   NCVO: National Council of Voluntary Organisations; PHAB: Physically Handicapped and Abled Bodied; RNID: Royal National Institute for the Deaf.

comments /contributions would be submitted to the FYD Trustees (and the Charity Commissioners when the time was right), for their immediate information and consideration.

After outlining what had happened between my secretary and myself and the decision-making processes leading up to and including the Trustees meeting on the 4th July, Craig opined that from the evidence tabled, the Trustees had not followed correct grievance procedures. It was the view of the DYAG that my secretary was accountable to me and that the Chair of Trustees should have referred her to me to resolve matters. Finally, the DYAG felt it was wrong that the Trustees had not made any attempt to discuss the problem or resolve matters between staff before making their decision not to renew my contract.

Evelyn asked Craig to remind the volunteers present that she had not lost confidence in me. She was in favour of giving me a chance, and wanted to make it clear that she had every confidence in my ability to direct the Trust, if I were given the right support.

Comments and questions were made open to the floor, and Craig read out three submissions from the absent Trustees

Trustee 1: 'I fail to see how such a confidential matter can be aired at such a public meeting! Currently the business of the non-renewal of Mrs. Rosie's contract lies in the hands of all Trustees.'

Trustee 2: 'Would you please advise Craig that in my role as a Trustee, I am accountable to the Charity Commissioners and would certainly not consider discussing matters of such a confidential nature in a public forum or contemplate breaking the confidences of my fellow Trustees'.

Trustee 3: 'I do not think it is wise at the present time for you to receive my comments and reasons with regard to the non-renewal of Mrs. Morag Rosie's contract of employment. This is for the best interests of your Youth Deaf Action Group and not myself'.

Past and present volunteers had also submitted written comments:

Denis Uttley – 'In our opinion, Mrs. Uttley and I feel the argument won't get you very far. FACTS – investigated. Authenticated and presented by an INDEPENDENT COMMITTEE OF ENQUIRY – is what would seem to be needed first of all'.

Volunteer – 'I have known Morag for 15 years and this period covers the real beginnings of the developments of FYD – a project that has grown from strength to strength over recent years. This growth is the direct result of

Morag's enthusiasm and hard work together with the help of volunteers who were themselves motivated by Morag Rosie.'

Ex-Director of RNID – 'I feel that I must write in support of Mrs. Rosie. When I was Director of RNID I had regular contact with her, particularly as the RNID gave significant financial help to FYD over a number of years, it was the special role and initiative of Morag Rosie that gave confidence to RNID in its support to FYD. The unique of involvement of volunteers in a wide programme of activity for young deaf people is something which came about as a result of Morag Rosie's special talents and hard work.'

Volunteer – 'As we had young FYD lodgers and we see improvements at the end of their stay with us. Whenever we call to see the Rosie's, Morag was always out at meetings, etc., during her off-duty hours. She gave herself wholeheartedly to this FYD project.'

Craig gave everyone present the opportunity to table comments / contributions / questions. This is a summary of the items that were raised:

Supporting statements of my character and leadership:
- Hearing staff followed up the written testimonials presented and vouched that if it had not been for me, they wouldn't have been encouraged to join and work for FYD and called for my reinstatement

The FYD Constitution
- FYD did not seem to be a very democratic organisation and it was insisted upon that FYD must get its Constitution in order so that this situation would not happen again.
- Questions were asked if the appointment of Trustees was for life. This was indeed the case and so it was felt that a signed document of letter of support in favour of me was not going to be enough because on the legal side, the Trustees appeared to have more power and were described as 'figureheads'. The constitution was unsatisfactory and an appeal should be made to the Trustees to work towards a solution.
- It was made clear, from questioning, that I had, on earlier occasions put forward my proposals for constitutional change at Trustees meetings but to no avail. The opinion was that the Trustees were at fault and that they had been incompetent in allowing the situation to get out of hand.

Grievance procedures
- It was felt that Trustees' decisions were badly planned and unnecessary.
- Evelyn was asked if the Director had the same rights as well as the

workers. Evelyn referred to the Employment Protection Act, and stated that the contract would be expected to continue as long as funding was there. She also stressed that there was no procedure with regard to a vote of 'No Confidence'. There was never any question of my work being unsatisfactory. As a Trustee, she could not see, on the whole, where I had gone wrong in my work with FYD.

- People were concerned that by not following the grievance procedure, the Trustees had broken my contract and the Trustees should be asked to explain why they had not followed procedures. It was also suggested that a lawyer from the Legal Centre should be brought in for a meeting to be set up with the FYD Trust.

Protocols of working in a Deaf/hearing environment

- The problem with hearing staff taking phone calls and relaying information on behalf of deaf colleagues appeared to be a core issue that required staff training and clarification of roles and responsibilities for working in a deaf/hearing environment.
- An example was given when a hearing person called the FYD Centre to speak to Morag, via her secretary, and felt that the conversation hadn't been relayed / interpreted properly.
- A volunteer who had previously worked at the FYD Centre with 6 other DHSS volunteers was concerned that all staff were now working under stressful conditions trying to sustain a high level of operations with only two volunteers on hand to support them.

People called for an Independent Committee of Inquiry

- Volunteers shared their experiences of working at the FYD Centre and how they were frustrated with my secretary's manners towards colleagues and she should not have gone straight to the Chair of Trustees without consulting with me first. This needed looking at.
- People wanted to understand why the Trustees had reacted to me in this way and only an inquiry could do this.
- An enquiry was considered as being the fairest way to understand both sides of the story, as trustees might have based their decisions on information unknown, with information concerning my position as Director that had not been shared.

The consensus was that a meeting with the Trustees was needed:

- It was important to ensure that the meeting "did not need to push the Trustees hard" as it would make things worse not better. Would such a meeting harm FYD? One of the members of staff declared that they had indeed spoken to the Chair of Trustees since the incident and expressed their concern that a wrong decision was being made and that I should be reinstated and appealed to him to have a meeting to mediate things.

- A Working Party meeting with the Trustees would allow them to justify their decision making and try to settle this difficult matter, to avoid having to take matters through legal routes and employment tribunals, which would not be in the best interest of FYD as I was also reluctant to take things that far.
- It was put to the floor, that once an amicable and compromising solution was reached, I would fight 'tooth and nail' for a radical change within FYD structures, policies and protocols for the 'sake of the next generation of young people." It was expressed that FYD was about 'friendship' and that real friendship was about moving forwards on the basis of 'listening' to one another and not taking a 'holier than thou' stance.
- A Working Party was selected from representatives of the DYAG, FYD Volunteers an supporters to meet with the Trustees

I was asked to conclude the meeting and I took the opportunity to tell everyone present that it was encouraging to know that from that point onwards I would have friends supporting me and I gave grateful thanks to everyone for their support.

10th September

Ken and I attended two meetings that turned out on the whole to be quite positive. First of all we met with Marcia Punnell, a barrister, who agreed to represent me if the matter went to Appeal or Industrial Tribunal. Marcia also advised me to speak to my solicitor to check the formal procedures for instigating such legal challenges. The main aim of those actions was to get me reinstated as the Director of FYD. Nothing else would seem to be satisfactory. Marcia was once the Chairperson of the Free Representational Unit (FRU) and was prepared to take on the case for personal reasons.

Our second meeting was to see how we were to maintain our relationship with the main funders of FYD. One of the successful aspects of FYD's long relationships with funders was that we maintained a frequent dialogue with key contact people, outside of formal obligations, in order that people could fully understand our work and our ambitions. To this end we met with Mr. Peter Clyne, an Assistant Director at the ILEA, where Edna Mathieson also accompanied us.

After outlining our situation, I asked Mr. Clyne if the ILEA should be informed of FYD's current situation. Peter felt that it was not necessary at that stage. He wished to remain unbiased but was ready to ask the appropriate questions when the time was right. The solemnity of this meeting brought home the importance of the fact that public money, from the ILEA and DHSS was being used to support FYD's work and that they should be concerned about FYD's future and its administration of those funds.

19th September
Working Party Group Meeting

The purpose of the meeting was to discuss and prepare for a meeting with the Trustees. Ken, Edna and I also updated everyone on the meetings held on 10th September with the barrister and the ILEA.

The discussion that followed included concerns about the FYD constitution that was allowing trustees to hold their position for life and so whatever the outcome of the present deliberations, this needed to be addressed, perhaps reducing the term of office to three year maximum before applying for re-election. We realised that the constitution needed to be revised at the earliest opportunity.

The whole episode was recognised as a 'learning curve' for us all, and it stressed how important POWER and POLITICAL awareness training was becoming for deaf people, if they were to take on strategic and senior roles within organisations.

Ken and I reassured everyone at the meeting that when we met with the barrister and the ILEA, they were made very aware of the strength of support that FYD and I had from its DYAG, volunteers and supporters – that they were aware of the actions being taken by the Working Group. Nobody had any idea what the trustees were feeling about the level of support being shown for FYD and we had no idea of any new developments.

The tone and contents of a letter to the trustees to request a meeting was discussed at length. The Working Group wanted to make it clear to the trustees, that although there were strong feelings about the decisions that they had made, people wanted to give them all possible opportunities to put across their side of the situation.

It was agreed that Edna Mathieson would be one of the representatives to meet the trustees, so that the working party had additional benefit of her knowledge and experience as well as demonstrating a balance of deaf and hearing representation.

It was also agreed that the minutes of the meeting on the 5th September would not be sent with the letter because it contained views that were highly critical of the trustees and this would not help the working party's case which was trying to take a neutral approach in its dialogue with the trustees.

30th September

The Trustees replied in writing to the Working Party's letter:

Dear Mr. Crowley

Thank you for your letter dated 22nd September and the contents were noted and discussed during the Trustees meeting on the same day. I have been asked to write to you on behalf of the Trustees.

We all feel that the matter of proposed delegation should wait until Mrs. Rosie's appeal against the non-renewal of her contract has been heard by us. You will be informed of the outcome of the Trustees; decision in due course.

The Trustees do appreciate your concern greatly, and hopes that the situation surrounding the FYD Trust will soon be resolved.

4th October
Craig replied to the Trustees on behalf of the Working Group:

Dear …

Your reply to the letter of which the FRIENDS of DYAG/FYD wrote to you still leaves most of us completely in the dark as to what is happening with regard to Morag Rosie's position and the future of FYD.

As you are deaf yourself, you will know only too well that most deaf people suffer all their lives from being left out and kept in the dark as others do not wish to include them! Invariably, it is hearing people's thoughtlessness and inability to understand the 'psychology of deafness', which is responsible for this. What surprises many of us is that you as a Trustee and a deaf person cannot see the enormous harm being done not only to Morag Rosie, but to other young deaf people, your own reputation and to the Trust itself!

Rumours around, because of lack of information, that the Chairperson of FYD is using his power as a hearing person and a Justice of Peace to manipulate you, Morag and others. There is a strong feeling among many young deaf people and volunteers that the present chairperson should resign as they have NO confidence in him. This is all very unfortunate as at the beginning of his involvement with FYD he seemed to have the potential of being the right kind of hearing person to be involved with such important developments. What went wrong and what should we be doing about it?

We know you are a Trustee-in-law but perhaps you should be reminded that we have been in many ways responsible for building up this Trust, as responsible deaf people together, do not let us destroy the Trust. Much of the success so far has been built on co-operation and mutual respect.

Can we get together soon so that we can avoid some unpleasant things happening in the future?

10th October
Following the correspondence, the Trustees agreed to meet with the Working Group on the 10th October. As we assembled for the meeting, Craig informed us that the Trustees had decided to resign en masse (with the Exception of Evelyn) because they were unable to maintain quorate attendances at meetings due to Evelyn's continued non-attendance.

We met this news all with jubilation and relief. I was reinstated and went back to work with the task of finding our new trustees.

To conclude this episode, I have reflected on it numerous times over the years and feel that there are some very important lessons to be learnt:

- The importance of transparent Constitutional governance that enables a clear and constructive working relationship between charity trustees and its management/staff that facilitates inevitable power struggles in a constructive way.
- Deaf organisations that are deaf-led have to ensure that they implement unique protocols that ensure clarity of roles between deaf and hearing staff such as the correct protocols for using the telephone when calls are interpreted.
- Stakeholders are vital to organisations; our experience has taught us that organisations that claim to represent young people should ensure that they are actively involved in serving the organisations that are set up to support them.

5

Leadership and Training, Projects and Young People (1987- 2000)

I n 1987, Evelyn was recruited as Co-Director to work alongside me in a demonstrative deaf/hearing partnership, which would permeate the philosophy of the organisation at every level.

One of the first things Evelyn and I created was a Development Plan for 1988-1995 that included a review of FYD's progress up to that point. The workload had grown steadily since I was appointed and we now had 14 full or part-time staff, of which 50% were deaf. We were organising almost 40 projects every year across the breadth of the country and with the establishment of our London and Birmingham offices, we were starting to develop local programmes.

Table 1: Analysis of participants and helpers who attended FYD projects 1980 -1987									
		Participants				Helpers			
Year	No of Projects	D	PH	H	Total	D	PH	H	Total
1980	2	25	14	20	59	7	9	10	26
1981	8	36	33	28	97	13	10	7	30
1982	12	156	35	60	251	30	50	7	87
1983	20	397	77	191	665	72	75	45	192
1984	41	1129	467	399	1995	178	78	201	457
1985	31	1056	336	305	1697	80	56	72	208
1986	29	904	1078	340	2322	61	75	122	258
1987	33	1212	897	350	2459	93	103	125	321
	176	4915	2937	1693	9545	534	456	589	1579

(Note: D – Deaf, PH – Partially Hearing, H – Hearing)

The above table shows the number of projects developed and delivered between 1980-87 and the numbers of participants and helpers involved. This was some workload and it's important to note that whilst the projects were organised by our office staff, they were supervised and carried through to fruition by the young people themselves.

It was on the basis of our Development Plan that we started to work strategically in cycles of three to five years. For the next 14 years or so, we continued to develop, evaluate and redesign our activities, bringing in new people with new ideas. In this chapter I want to describe our developments in three key areas of our work: Leadership and training, Projects and Young people.

Leadership and Training

In 1988, we received a grant from the Carnegie (UK) Trust to appoint Craig as our Research and Development Officer based at Bulmershe College of Higher Education/Reading University. His part-time Administration and Research assistant was Mark Harvey who, like Craig, had also been President of the College Student Union. Following a period of research and the testing of new thinking, the revised National Training programme was re-launched in November 1990.

The programme was launched with a cadre of trainee leaders who wanted take responsibility for tutoring and leading the courses, starting in the first instance with Initiative Training. They were; Charlotte Moulton Thomas, Malcolm Sinclair, Mark Wheatley, Jayne House, Mandy Loach (now Crump), Rachel Williams, Damian Barry, Dennis Hodgkins, Sharon Hirshman, Janet Wardle (now Wardle-Peck) and Jemima Lambert (now Bouy).

Whilst these earnest individuals proceeded to build up a head of steam, Evelyn and I had attended an Industrial Society function in London, where Terry Thompson, a former CEO of PHAB was the guest speaker.

> I was fascinated to see one lady in the audience signing to another. In conversation afterwards, we found that we shared a common philosophy – to create a society in which people who were disadvantaged (mainly by society itself) had the opportunity to develop their own potential as both participants and leaders. Their ideas were very similar to PHAB, but instead of barriers to wheelchairs it was barriers to communication, which created the problems. Many activities excluded young deaf people, not because of any lack on their part, but because teachers, leaders and managers had not bothered to develop the right communication skills or provide support in activities.
>
> Like most people, I could not resist the enthusiasm and persuasion of the 'dynamic duo'!
>
> (Terry Thompson)

Surely enough, our *enthusiasm and persuasion* resulted in Terry mentoring Craig with some one to one support, where he shared his extensive experience and

The Dynamic Duo: Morag Rosie and Evelyn Carter. (FYD)

helped to progress further Craig's natural instinct for training and management development:

> Of course, I was learning as much as he was, mainly in the field of communication and the needs of young deaf people. This grounding from Craig, and meetings with Morag and Evelyn, where I learnt how deaf and hearing partnership really worked, laid a great foundation for what was to follow.
>
> We were both enthusiastic about how our skills could come together and my one-day a month soon became two, then two a week and before I knew it I closed my fledging training agency and joined FYD full-time. It's funny how FYD does that to you isn't it?
>
> (Terry Thompson)

Terry was appointed as our third Director with responsibility for the organisation's Professional Leadership Training. Up to this point, the Leadership programme wasn't formally documented as such and so one of Terry's first tasks was to put together the over-arching doctrine and training curriculum with all the supporting materials required.

In March 1991, the Training Offices were moved to Ladywood in Birmingham and one of the staff based there was the irrepressible Damian Barry. Over the next five years, Damian and Terry further developed the National Training programme (NTP) and created the role of Ambassadors. We appointed Damian as Head of Training in 1992.

By 1993, we were aiming the NTP at deaf and hearing people aged 16+; it was delivered over a course of weekends with opportunities to get practical experience in all parts of the FYD programme. It comprised four sections:

Section 1 – Participation training – This element of the programme included sports festivals, drama, art and outings etc with the participation ratio of 3:1. This introduced young people to new activities to build their communication skills and boosted confidence for participants whose ages ranged from 8 to 25 years old. Within this section, we also started to pilot our family projects to support both Parents and children together.

Section 2 – Initiative training weekend – In order to take the initiative or to make appropriate, informed, decisions, a young person needs to be able to combine; language skills, knowledge, experience, access to information, access to communication, confidence, encouragement and positive self-worth. In our experience, many deaf people were denied the opportunity to develop these skills. Others may not be given the opportunity or encouragement to use them effectively.

Section 3- Leadership Training – Two weekends known as Part 1 and Part 2 where we trained young people to take the lead in FYD activities.

Section 4- was the popular name for further training and work experience known as the *'Ambassador Programme'*. Ambassadors were young people aged 20-30 years old who had completed all four sections of the NTP and were called 'Ambassadors' because they qualified to represent FYD and take responsibility, on behalf of the organisation, for events in their own geographical areas. In the same way that government ambassadors do for their own countries.

In addition to all of this, we had 'CATS' – Community Action training. This was for volunteers who were mainly unemployed, who were given work experience opportunities with FYD in their local area. Here, they helped to organise projects as Ambassadors or act in a support role, helping young people and promoting FYD. This was supported by funding to pay for the volunteers expenses from the Opportunities for Volunteering programme, which we had now been running for ten years.

Although the training programme was popular with the participants, we had to work very hard at promoting it. In our review of 1993, we were expecting to see an increase in numbers joining the NTP as a result of the promotional activities by our Ambassadors, led by Damian. Indeed, Terry was even looking at the concept of establishing a national training centre for integration and communication. We also looked ahead to 1995/6 and suggested that by then, the annual NTP would comprise 6 Initiative courses, 2 each of Leadership Parts 1 and 2 and one section 4 course.

For the NTP to have any credibility it needed to be run by Deaf people qualified as trainers. In a chance conversation with a Director from GlaxoSmithKline (GSK) at an *Employers Forum on Disability* meeting, Damian was asked why Deaf people were not coming forward for jobs in GSK. He explained that there was (and still is) a serious lack of confidence amongst young deaf people who did not believe that

Initiative Training, Rheidol Study Centre, Aberystwyth 1992 (FYD)

they were 'job worthy'. As a result we received a substantial donation from GSK to help create a pilot 12-week pre-vocational training programme.

The training was delivered by Damian and as a result, it was proved that with the right support, people could be empowered to believe that they are job worthy. At the same time, the pilot demonstrated that for deaf people to believe that they can play a role in the job market, they needed to see examples of other deaf leaders in the workplace.

Damian decided to lead by example and took the Institute for Personnel and Development (IPD) qualifications to show that it could be done. Another seven deaf and hearing members of staff then followed Damian's lead this up and gained the qualification for themselves. By 1997, we had seven deaf and one hearing trainers all qualified and so, with this capacity, FYD was able to expand out into the regions, promoting the NTP and delivering it through our network of Embassy Development Officers[1] and Ambassadors. Another outcome from this development was the creation of our internal 'Staff College"; a two year training programme specifically for FYD staff and its development workers. Our ambitions even extended to the possibility of opening an International Residential Training Centre by 1997, but this needed the not inconsiderable sum of £1 million.

We felt we had a good package that could also be offered to other organisations and thereby generate business revenue for FYD. We also wanted to offer Deaf Awareness training (DAT) to all, but at the time, we weren't sure of the demand and

1   See Chapter 6 – Embassies

so we concentrated on building a team first.

But by the end of 1994, we were not filling places on the pre-vocational training programme and our review of the NTP was taking longer than expected. We felt that training needs and organisational needs were constantly changing and that it would be best to take our time to achieve a full review. To help us do this, we reorganised our staffing and appointed two deaf people into senior roles; Damian as Director of Training and Claire Ingham, (nee Cummings) as Programme Manager.

For the next two years, our staff had to work extremely hard to ensure that our NTP courses were full. With the advent of the National Lottery, our traditional sources of funds were diminishing and so we took the reluctant decision to cut back on the staff training and public relations – to reduce the number of administrative trainees at East Grinstead from two to one. We also put our monthly cash-flow reviews under greater scrutiny and we also agreed to take on bank overdrafts providing we had the knowledge of incoming funds to cover them.

We had an agreement with the Princes' Trust to fund places on the NTP, but they too, were also being affected by the new elephant in the room, the National Lottery. They went on to change their policy to lower the age limits for supporting disabled people, since they had also seen a reduction in their own available funds after they lost heavily with investments in the Barings Bank collapse. Quite frankly it was chaos.

Damian, Claire and their teams were constantly reviewing the NTP to ensure that the training dovetailed well with the participation projects, so that the programme was more practice than theory. We were also examining the option of compulsory project experiences (similar to the Duke of Edinburgh Award scheme) that we could manage with our own limited resources and finances. We were also concerned that the principle of the deaf and hearing partnership was being lost, because people were also progressing too quickly through the NLT programme and not taking the time to reflect and appreciate the subtle undertones.

In December 1995, Terry resigned to take up work with the Deafax Trust, which was closer to his home and involved less travelling. Obviously this was better for him as it allowed him to spend more time at home with his family.

> I have so many memories of FYD... But most of all the friendship, and I hope, making some contribution to one of the most exciting and useful organisations I have ever known.
>
> (Terry Thompson)

We soldiered on with 14 trained Ambassadors and we were confident that we would soon have a pool of competent DAT trainers. We also prioritised a group of Ambassadors to be tasked with the delivery of the training programme itself.

We turned a corner in May 1996, when Damian successfully won two major funding applications. This enabled us to start implementing a new concept titled

Terry Thompson and Morag during a lighter moment. (FYD)

'Action Centred Development' which sat alongside the NTP. We appointed Mandy Crump (Training Manager) and Sue Barry (ACD Manager) who were to be supported by our Embassy Development Officers. The training was aimed at reinforcing the FYD Philosophy, which I considered to be our sacrosanct.

Action Centred Development or ACD was a youth development and peer support programme that focused on building better partnerships for young people. This innovative four-year programme aimed at training deaf and hearing volunteers, aged 18-25, as role models and mentors for young deaf people. In all, it trained 130 volunteers who coached or mentored 1,300 young people in their personal and social development – a considerable achievement, to say the least. Funding came from the Esmee Fairbairn Charitable Trust, the Department of Education and Employment (DfEE) and the National Lotteries Charities Board.

When we analysed the ACD programme, we were able to critically examine the 'working partnership between deaf and hearing people' that we had advocated so highly. In our competitive world, deaf people are often left behind due to the challenges of communication and the lack of skills of hearing people in communicating effectively with deaf people. We developed a framework of support and communication methods that enabled deaf and hearing people to form effective partnerships in order to work together. To achieve this working partnership, it isn't enough just to provide places or fill posts with deaf and hearing people, as consideration must be given to:

- Providing appropriate communication support to deaf people
- Providing 'voice over' support for hearing people
- Agreeing ground rules for communication before the start of each project
- Agreeing type and level of support
- Agreeing aims and objectives, or expectations, of project or event
- Accepting confidentiality
- Agreeing on positive criticism, if needs be
- Making allowances for inexperienced participants
- Following a model of good communication practices at all times (e.g. do not exclude anybody in a mixed group by choosing inappropriate communication methods)
- Ensuring that deaf and hearing people are fully involved at all times (discussions, suggestions, decision making, fact finding)
- Encouraging, nurturing and supporting each other at all times.

(Action Centred Development Programme 1996-1999 p9)

The development process of the ACD focused on empowering people. Empowerment is creating opportunities and it means people are resourced to gain control and responsibility over their lives, through being able to make choices and decisions from a position of knowledge and support. What made FYD's work unique and what differentiated it from many other organisations was that the training programme brought together young deaf and hearing people in a special, but equitable, partnership. The underlying principles were that:

- It enabled young deaf people to develop individually
- It increased their self confidence
- It included young deaf people by providing equal opportunities
- It helped young deaf people to achieve though life-long learning experiences
- It helped young deaf people play a full part as competent citizens with a real stake in society

(Action Centred Development Programme, 1996-1999 p12.)

Over the years, we learnt to meet the challenges of designing an in-house programme for a group of volunteers with different needs. We had to consider: the type of participant (deaf or hearing), a mix of communication methods (Sign language, signed English, lip-speaking, deaf-blind manual and spoken English) any learning difficulties and other aspects such as food requirements and allergies. From the deaf perspective, there are clear advantages of training and learning in small groups as it makes allowances for effective observation of group discussion, mobility and visual issues e.g. colour and movement for ease of communication between people.

From a hearing perspective, there may be some disadvantages – lack of knowledge and understanding of deaf issues (for those new to deaf culture) and the lack of signing skills. The course materials were also adapted to suit deaf people by giving more visual metaphors. We encouraged everyone to start by attending the Initiative training weekends, as this allowed people to appreciate the dynamics of regional communication differences in sign language, as well as English dialects, and people also brought along their different attitudes, experiences, learning styles and preferences. At this early stage we helped everyone to identify his or her individual learning styles according to the Kolb, Honey and Mumford principle. We also encouraged people to appreciate the dynamics of the different styles within the groups.

Learning Styles from Kolb and Honey and Mumford are based on the learning cycle using the participants experience (taking action); reflection (observing, gathering data and sharing feelings); conclusion (developing and understanding theories and concepts) and application (putting theory into practice). Honey & Mumford's theory suggests four types of learning style:

- Activist – 'get stuck in'
- Reflector – 'sleep on it'
- Theorist – 'fit theory'
- Pragmatist – 'get on with it'

Our experience demonstrated that for young deaf people, there was a preference for less theoretical learning and for a more practical application of new ideas and concepts.

Our Embassy Development Officers were undertaking training offered in the 'Staff College' and this was being reflected in their change of attitude towards training and management and the professionalisation of their work. We were also optimistic that the ACD with support from Olwyn Cupid (HMI)[2] would seek accreditation leading to recognised qualifications. We saw accreditation of the ACD and NTP as a way of raising the status of FYD and the long-term benefits would enable us to tap into more government funds.

By the end of the summer in 1996, we were operating from four Embassies and there was progress in registering the Training programme for accreditation with Warwickshire & Hinckley College, who had taken an interest in the Peer support elements of our programme, and we were also about to move into a joint Training Centre and Midlands Embassy in Nuneaton.

Doug Morgan from Reach[3] had been assisting Damian with a Staff Development

2   HMI: Her Majesties Inspectorate
3   REACH: An organisations connecting charities with skilled volunteers or interim support

Policy and his work was funded through the "Counselling, Empowering and Listening" grants scheme. Like a vast number of people who supported FYD over the years, Doug worked for 23 days but he only charged for six.

We met our targets for the first year of the Training and ACD programmes and some changes were made in the ACD course outline as it seemed the workload was becoming too 'heavy' for some. We needed a rethink. We knew this would not have a negative impact with our funders as all new pilots and ideas are there to allow for things to be trialed and changed.

In 1997, our Embassy Development Officers gained their IPD and NEBSM[4] professional qualifications and in our quest to continually create opportunities and recognise the work of Deaf people, we appointed Craig Crowley as one of our Vice Presidents.

In 1998/1999, our ACD programme recruited 42 volunteers and provided them with a total of 365 training days, which resulted in 420 deaf children and young people receiving peer support from our ACD volunteers. The NTP and the ACD were amalgamated and affiliated to the John Huskins model of personal development, which comprised seven stages:

- Levels 1–4   doing things for young people
- Level 5   working with young people
- Levels 6–7   doing things by young people

A former member of staff, John Walker held capacity development sessions with staff and participants to try and find ways of avoiding jargon when explaining the NTP to young deaf people who, invariably, would have limited language skills. By marrying the appropriate courses or events with the different stages, we were able to provide a continuous path of personal development though the FYD journey. With John's help on jargon-busting, we were able to create a more attractive package with which to launch the "Young Deaf People First" programme, which had the support of the Esmee Fairbairn Trust, Department for Education and Employment, Department of Health and the National Lottery. Angela Sew Hoy and Mandy Crump were appointed to write up the evaluation report on the ACD[5].

When Mandy took maternity leave in 1999/2000, we drew up a freelance contract to bring John Walker back into the FYD fold, to lead workshops and training courses until the vacancy of Training Manager could be filled. Our attempts to gain accreditation for the training had moved on to work with Chester College, looking to create modules of 120 hours of learning through participation in FYD courses and projects, to demonstrate experiential learning that could be added to portfolios. If passed, the accreditation of the Young Deaf People First programme could be accredited to the Certificate of Higher Education.

---

4   NEBSM: National Examining Board in Supervisory Management
5   Action Centred Development Programme 1996-1999

By 2000, we had also won funding to deliver training to parents and families with an Early Intervention programme which was headed by Alistair Wright, who had come from the NDCS with 9 years experience of working with families. Our Early intervention work was unique because it worked with deaf and hearing parents who had deaf children but, ALSO, worked with Deaf parents who only had hearing children.

Unfortunately, we were still unable to accredit the Young Deaf People First programme because it required an assessor and a verifier which we did not have the resources for and the pressure from a lack of incoming funds, meant we had to put that next stage on hold until we were ready.

Projects

With the increase in demand, our projects had been extended, year on year. The successful development of the leadership training had enabled us to increase the volume of individual events. Just before the conflict broke out between the Trustees, and myself the RNID had reviewed our work and although they were complimentary, they were also correct and arrogantly so, about one of my greatest frustrations; that we could not reach every deaf child in the UK:

'The aim of FYD is to improve the prospects of every deaf child whatever their need, from the chance to excel at some sporting event to educational opportunities and employment prospects or merely to make new friends and it has failed so far only in as much as it has not reached every deaf child; in mitigation it can point to the many hundreds it has reached.'

(RNID 1986)

All our projects contained elements of education. Although they were designed to be enjoyed by the participants, they were also providing opportunities to increase personal skills, to learn about the needs of other people, to extend the individuals first hand experiences, sharing knowledge with others and developing reading and language skills.

The combination of stimulating the mind, the sense of achievement and the ease of communication often showed dramatic increases in linguistic skills. Our experience showed that Deaf children and young people were sometimes unaware of how much information that had been missing within their 'ordinary' environment and we were concerned that this was seriously impairing their powers of understanding and decision-making.

In our Development Plan for 1987-1995 we talked about the need for an effective counselling service that included deaf and hearing counsellors. There was a lack of provision to meet the needs in regards to effective integration, education, careers advice, sex education and general youth guidance. We all felt that as a minority group, deaf people needed at least as much, if not more counselling facilities if they

76

Midland Sports Festival, 1990 (FYD)

were to make the transition from adolescent to adulthood.

Surely as we had planned, our team of staff, volunteers and the number of people on our training programme increased further and the portfolio of projects remained our staple diet, our bread and butter. But, things did not always stay this way. As we moved into the mid- 1990s, the landscape of provision for young people began to get more commercialised and our projects began to lack support as families began to consider the cost of sending their children to our events.

Millfield in particular was becoming very expensive and we dispatched Ken Carter off to Somerset to try and re-negotiate a new deal to keep the costs affordable. Meanwhile, we began to look for alternative residential/sports venues like universities etc. Our international reputation was growing as more individuals and groups from overseas were getting involved in projects like Millfield. It was most unfortunate when we could not afford run the Millfield summer course in 1994. It was just so expensive and so we stopped it indefinitely. We had to contact all the families who had pre-booked and offer them places on our Bude project, which was an altogether different experience, even though it offered sport and adventure opportunities on the beautiful north coast of Cornwall.

Whilst Millfield and other sports specific projects were excellent in the development of young people, those who made the switch to Bude and our

Bude Dragon Boats (FYD)

Activity briefing at Bude (FYD)

Bude Management Training (FYD)

smaller adventure week in Keswick (Lake District), later realised that the adventure projects were much more challenging and offered wider opportunities for personal development which were altogether more psychologically and physically demanding; especially hurling yourself off the side of a sheer cliff-face backwards with only a slender rope for support. If that's not character building then what is!?

Adventure International hosted the annual Bude Week for us. In the beginning, we had a straightforward programme of adventure activities, but as our relationship developed and our numbers grew, the programme was divided into age-appropriate activities which provided specific experiential learning for the NTP volunteers as project managers and supervisors. We also developed a management training course involving challenging physical and mental tasks for those aged 18+.

1994/1995 saw us extend our presence beyond England and through our Embassy network we were beginning to deliver projects in Wales and Scotland and at Bude '94, we hosted a group of young people and their leaders from Switzerland. The popularity of this international perspective encouraged people to demand that we developed this further.

The Operations team reported a very favourable response from Scotland to our projects and so we proceeded to organise a video production taster day and a sports festival. We were developing a network that reached out through schools, local organisations and we took a view that we would have enough Scottish volunteers available to help us deliver the activities planned. Things were looking good.

We continued to face the challenge of financial viability as some projects were markedly low in numbers and our project team was under pressure to discontinue them. But my argument was that the courses were not only benefitting the participants, but they remained valuable training opportunities for our leaders. We focused our promotion and recruitment through the London/South East Embassy because we still had a large deaf population density in that region.

We piloted our first family intervention weekends and in our reviews we acknowledged that we needed to provide more detailed briefings for the volunteer supervisors who were looking after the children's activities, whilst parents were in their own workshops. The most significant outcome of this was to prepare our volunteers by holding workshops around the relevant parts of the 1989 Children's Act and its implications for their roles.

We had 220 people attending Bude '95 and we had to manage the demands of the children and young people within the health and safety requirements of Adventure International and thanks to our training programme and our project leaders, we established a very good rapport with the centre staff and generally they were very supportive of our groups needs. The centre Director had even taken the time out to go around all the local shops and businesses in the town to encourage owners, managers and their staff to become more deaf-aware before our arrival!

> From the Centre's perspective, a booking for a group including 200 deaf people would seem at first sight to be any sensible Director's idea of a nightmare! That's 20 groups of young people taking part in ten potentially lethal activities who may not understand the instructor or hear the shouts of help or warnings and may find communication a problem. Or, from the reverse view, 45 trained, qualified instructors who suddenly find they can't communicate. Frightened because they must attempt a totally unfamiliar way of putting over their sport, perhaps involving danger to the group.
>
> Yet it works, because in practice it's two groups of people who because of the possible dangers break through all the barriers of communication in the shortest possible time! So intent are both sides on success that all the 'politics of handicap' disappear. It may be impossible to teach someone to sign in a week but by simplifying the system, in four days everyone is locked together in intense conversation. Every success at communication forms a bond much stronger than any I have seen in the 15 years I have been running the centre. Roll on August and the FYD/Adventure International Experience '95!
>
> (Keith Marshall, Managing Director of Adventure International, Bude)

Bude required a volunteer group of 40 people, who had given up a week of their time willingly as leaders and communicators. No mean undertaking and some found the pressure of the week very demanding. But we knew we were doing the right things as we were getting enquiries from families for the next year as soon as their children were home! Feedback from our fieldwork indicated that people regarded FYD as 'being good for young people and training'.

We also took the initiative to reposition our brand to establish FYD as a youth and training organisation, rather than as sporting one as this was how we felt

Art Competition 1995 (FYD)

people still regarded us. The project programme had less emphasis on sport as we introduced a more varied choice of activities. We attempted to break new ground in the South East by delivering an Arts & Crafts programme in parallel to the sports activities at the 1995 Crystal Palace Festival. With these new activities aimed at 5 – 7 year olds, we were able to attract 250 participants to the festival and the new opportunities were received with enthusiasm.

Using the evaluation of our pilot to provide early intervention weekends for families, we secured funding for three years from the Department of Health and Linkelley, which ran from 1997-2000. We had a family weekend at Charterhouse School and local projects in the four embassy regions. These were successful projects enabling deaf and hearing families to discover the potential of their children and by the end of the funding term, we were working with 50 families directly.

Before and during the early days of the merger with NDCS. I thoroughly enjoyed co-planning and delivering with the brilliant Mandy Crump on several family weekends for parents of deaf children. It was a challenge to manage conversations between parents with very different ideas about how they wanted to raise their children. We aimed to convey the message that looking at adult deaf role models could help, as well as thinking about things from the child's social and emotional as well as intellectual development.

(Sarah Playforth)

Young People

For me, FYD will always be about the young people we represented. What young people achieved was the indicator by which we measured the success of our work. Therefore it was important to me that we allowed them to be part of our decision-making; the shaping of our philosophy, polices and programming.

At first, we were able to do this through the *Opportunities for Volunteering* scheme. We enabled young people to design, build, promote, recruit and support each other on activities that were of interest to them and their peers. We backed this up with the National Leadership Training programme, which they also managed and led.

The FYD Trust was a national charity where a large proportion of its management team under the age of 40 years old. Those young people were in post, variously, as Director, Manager and in sole charge of Embassy offices. It is quite amazing when you think of it; I don't think there was any youth charity worldwide at the time that could claim to have had **57%**[6] of its management workforce occupied by people under the age of 40. I don't think that is something that has ever happened since and it is something that was not capitalised on more assertively by FYD at the time.

If I had written this book immediately after the closure of the Trust, it would have been rather different from the one you are reading today because we would not have been able to include the testimonials that demonstrate the power of its 14-year legacy. I want this book to be a tool and an inspiration for something new; for young people in the future.

> I can never forget my FYD days back in 1988 with all the leadership training and volunteering. FYD gave me my very first job based in London looking after the needs of Deaf people in Lewisham.
>
> (Jemima Bouy)

I have been asked if we took a risk with young people in such responsible roles. FYD placed a great emphasis on empowering young deaf/hearing people to run the organisation, which worked out well, but perhaps we could have had provided our Embassy Development Officers with better mentoring and support? Stuart Harrison remembers that when I took on Craig and himself in the 1980s, they were very heavily supervised. He dreads to think what they would have got up to if after a couple of years, I had sent them away to run our Embassy offices without supervision. He believes they would have created chaos for the Trust!

> In the 1980s, everything was run from the East Court offices in East Grinstead, things were manageable. When I think back to those times, Craig and I were kept on a tight "professional' leash by you!

---

6   Based on the staff profile on 9th June 1999 as recorded in Minutes of Staff meeting.

I wanted to laugh when Stuart mentioned that I put himself and Craig on a tight leash! Being a big bully I was only a human being with a care for young people! To think of it, it was a blessing that Craig and Stuart decided to go to University and pursue their own career paths.

Employing young people as Embassy Development Officers also had the positive impact of enabling FYD to build working relationships with its stakeholders as both staff and stakeholders were of the same age/generation.

I still meet people who say the best time they had was during the FYD period.
That is when I can say I did a good job. That gave me the skills for my future.
(Marcel Hirshman, SE Embassy Development Officer)

FYD was successful because it fulfilled the dream of seeing young people ready themselves for the future with confidence and with experience under their belt that enabled them to choose what they wanted to do with their lives. On top of this, they returned to help the Trust in later years and gained insight that enabled them to take up career challenges that met their thirst experience and responsibility.

I would agree, to some degree, that investing in young people is risky but we militated against any difficulties by developing "Staff College". The college worked, BUT, did that come at a cost to FYD? I would say that FYD should be very proud that 57% of its management comprised young people. The 40-year FYD management 'trainee' proved that young people can take on demanding roles with responsibility for others, providing of course that they are supported by back-office teams with the greater experience, to ensure that this way of working does not have a negative impact on the sustainability of the organisation itself.

In March 1993 we established a 'Council' (Advisory Group) to provide opportunities for direct input into policy development and where appropriate, the management of FYD. To represent the views of deaf and hearing young people – to share in the development of the Trust; to advance integration; to share and learn from the experiences and to develop committee and participation skills amongst its members. The Council membership consisted of one Trustee; up to six Ambassadors; up to 4 corporate friends and other individuals, all appointed with the approval of the Trustees.

6

Outreaching

Australia

In the summer of 1993, at the invitation of Margaret Imrie, Damian travelled to Melbourne and Sydney to deliver a series of training workshops based on our National Leadership Training programme and to publicise the aims, objectives and work of FYD. Margaret had experienced FYD on a previous visit to the UK and was keen to see the same provision established in Australia. In the conclusion of his field report, Damian said that the visit had helped people piece together the differing parts of the FYD jigsaw into a cohesive whole.

The feedback from the training and presentations delivered by Damian indicated that there was potential to start a programme and it certainly captured the imagination of the, internationally renowned, Deaf leader John Lovett who was so impressed by the 'tremendous impact' with the Melbourne Deaf community, that he extended his scheduled visit to England (en route to the Sofia World Games for the Deaf) to meet Hamish and myself. He then travelled up to Birmingham to see Damian at the Training Centre and observe the Initiative training at 'The Chandlery'.

> After the visit, John Lovett (Community Services Manager) became much more understanding that the Training Programme does not threaten the very existence of the Deaf community but can be seen as enhancing harmony between different kinds of deafness and producing leaders with positive attitudes and creating positive awareness of deafness.
>
> (Damian Barry in 'Australian Trip (3rd-25th June 1993) Report' p 5)

Towards the end of 1994, reports to the FYD-UK Board and Council implied that the Australians appeared to have lost momentum in setting up their local version of FYD. As it had been a while since any of us had been there, we were hoping that things would pick up.

In April/May 1995, I visited Australia and New Zealand where I caught up with Evelyn on her sabbatical. My intentions were to give support to our ambassadors Margaret in Australia and Chris Blum in New Zealand.

In Sydney our energies were completely drained by Margaret and her contacts, all of whom were dying to know more and more about the FYD Philosophy and the latest developments from the Training programme. Clearly, Damian had done

Australia (John Wheeler)

a good job of laying down the foundations when he was there two years previously.

The timing of our visit was right for giving moral support; Margaret felt that she could now see the way forward as to how to positively start FYD full support from Doug Powers (Deaf), the CEO of the Adult Education Centre for Deaf and Hard of Hearing persons (AET), their board members and other individuals.

We advised Margaret to wait a while before setting up FYD proper and to work with Doug and Damian to develop training courses under the wing of the AET on a voluntary basis. Doug, Anthony Hogan (Hearing) and Stephen Nicholson (Deaf) were planning to visit the UK to meet FYD staff and volunteers. Margaret was planning a visit for January 1996 to get a 'recharge' before getting things off the ground in Australia.

New Zealand

Christoph Blum and his wife Sarah, a deaf couple from New Zealand, had visited the UK in 1990. On their 'tour' they were particularly keen to see what they could learn from the UK Deaf community and take back to their peers in New Zealand. They visited national deaf organisations to understand their work and attended the BDA Congress in Brighton, where they saw for themselves the importance of human rights and political engagement.

After reading through a copy of the FYD Newsletter they decided to 'have a look' and enrolled on an Initiative training course in 1991; where they were inspired by the work of Damian Barry and John Walker. They enrolled as project volunteers and Chris quickly worked his way through the training programme right up to Ambassador level.

> In the 1980s/90s there were no real opportunities provided for leadership or team building in NZ so participating in the FYD programme in the UK was something I had never encountered. It was an awesome experience.
>
> I gained an insight into other peoples perspectives and attitudes, learnt

through partnerships with Hearing and Deaf and discovered a vast range of communication methods. My confidence grew.

Being able to access a course without barriers was liberating. Through the course I noticed more doors to life opened up for me than ever before. It triggered aspirations and dreams of wanting to bring back to NZ the wonderful knowledge I had gained and share it with the Deaf community as I knew back home we were lacking this calibre of training.

(Chris Blum)

Chris knew that he had to take his new knowledge and skills back to New Zealand where there were increasing concerns about the problems of Deaf youth. Despite early indications highlighted by Ian Smith, a Teacher of the Deaf who, in 1977, addressed a 'Youth at Risk' seminar in Wellington where he explained that deaf youth were at risk from a lack of training for jobs, an unwillingness of employers to train them, public reluctance to learn to communicate with them, overprotection by teachers and parents and poor examples set by older deaf people. By the time Chris was well into his FYD training in 1992, Kim Robinson spoke at the New Zealand Association of the Deaf (NZAD) AGM about the challenge of a marginalized deaf youth who were living rough, taking drugs and, in some instances, committing suicide.[1]

On his return to New Zealand in 1993, Chris learnt that the NZAD were trying to appoint someone as a Youth Coordinator to tackle some of the major concerns identified. But he knew that if he was going to take on the role, he needed to be better prepared. So he persuaded the NZAD to pay for both himself and Sarah to return to the UK and in the space of four and a half weeks, in February and March 1994, they travelled through England and Scotland visiting a range of FYD projects, training courses and strategic meetings to both understand the operational rationale of FYD and how things could be implemented. This tour concluded when he met with our Operations Marketing Manager and myself to confirm plans for FYD New Zealand (FYD-NZ).

On his return home, he quickly set about making plans for the first Initiative training weekend and he started in his new role on 1st August 1994. We released two of our Training Ambassadors, Janet Wardle and Sue Barry, to fly out to help Chris to run his first two Initiative weekends. He was also drafted in as a consultant to assist the Federation for Deaf Children with an Outdoor Pursuits camp. The first two years were a very busy time, touring throughout New Zealand, setting up events and training people.

Leadership training merged with Kiwis love of camps and outdoor living. The theoretical components of leadership were aligned with putting into practice

---

1   Chapter 15: *Talking Hands, Listening Eyes* page 195

on a real-time basis.

(Dugdale, P. in Talking Hands, Listening Eyes pp 213-217)

When I visited New Zealand in 1995, I was impressed with the way Chris had been working. He had devised a clear strategy and FYD New Zealand was progressing at the right pace with the excellent support of his CEO, Tricia Fitzgerald. Everyone I met was full of praise for Christopher's own leadership, particularly Bridget Brown who wrote:

Chris is a terrific asset here. He really has a heart for young people and does FYD proud; his flamboyant presentation and main manner are really winning converts. He is doing a good job of representing FYD here, and creates a lot of good relationships along the way.

It was great to meet FYD groups in Auckland, Hamilton, Palmerston North and Wellington. I was hit by their enthusiasm and motivation for the future of FYD in New Zealand. They had already gained theoretical and practical experience through the initiative training weekends run by Janet Wardle and Sue Barry and from acting as supervisors on projects. I want to take the opportunity here to repeat my praise for Janet and Sue who did a good job running the Initiative weekends in 1994 – Looking back on my experience then, I appreciate now, more than ever, that they had a difficult task, starting something completely new in a very different country.

Such was the impact of Chris' work that with positive 'discrimination' from Board members of the Deaf Association who had attended training, Tricia Fitzgerald requested that all 14 remaining Board members attend the next Weekend course so as to improve their understanding of teamwork which was, regrettably, lacking

Youth Camp with FYD – NZ (Chris Blum, far left) (courtesy of Chris Blum)

in their organisation.

This was an opportunity for Chris to gain more experience before being assessed by Damian as to his ability to run such courses solo. Chris' aim was to become a qualified trainer and was planning another visit to England.

I took time out to compare what was happening in Australia and New Zealand and I assessed that Chris had an advantage over Margaret because his brief as Youth Coordinator meant he was able to make full use of the FYD training programme, working on a full time basis accountable to the NZDA. Tricia was seeking a formal partnership with FYD-UK in order to form a strong bridge between the two organisations. Margaret was to progress on a smaller scale in her spare time, until she was in a position to set up an FYD organisation in Sydney (which we anticipated would take a year or two.)

This demonstrated to me at that time, that we needed to produce more trainers and leaders to cope with the growth of FYD not just in the UK, but the rest of the world – there were two nations on the map already. I suggested at my next Board meeting that we should be giving serious consideration to the establishment of the International Training Centre as part of our Three-year plan. I left this as a task for the FYD Directors to consider.

In 1997, the NZAD appointed their first Deaf manager when Damian and Sue travelled out with the intention of staying for two years to mentor FYD-NZ through a period of growth. With Damian in the role of Manager, Jennifer Brain was promoted to Council Development Manager and in July 1997 she travelled to visit the FYD-UK Bude week, FYD Offices, CACDP[2], RNID and BDA[3].

At the end of 1997, reshuffling some of the related roles within NZAD created the FYD-NZ team. The team comprised Jennifer Brain (FYD Manager, responsible for overseeing the development of FYD-NZ), Damian Barry (Consultant and Advisor), Elaine Sautia (hearing, Deputy FYD Manager), Chris Blum (FYD Trainer), Patrick Thompson (FYD Trainee Trainer) and Helen Keane (hearing, FYD Further Development and Literacy Coordinator)

To describe what FYD-NZ was trying to do, they explained how Damian spoke about FYD in terms of the positive and negative communication cycles:

2   CACDP: Council for the Advancement of Communication with Deaf People
3   BDA: British Deaf Association.

THE NEGATIVE COMMUNICATION CYCLE: is a process of failure and frustration – perhaps from poor education leading to poor communication, lack of understanding, bad attitudes, resentment, lack of confidence and isolation.

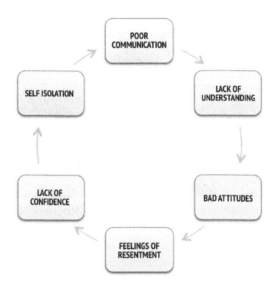

THE POSITIVE COMMUNICATION CYCLE: Is the process of transforming the individual by satisfactory communication leading to understanding, better attitudes, inclusion in the community and happiness.

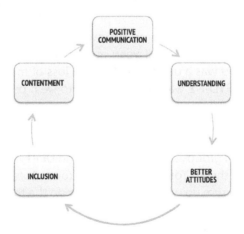

To achieve Positive Cycles, FYD-NZ in 1997 was developing a programme to include people of all ages, both deaf and hearing Impaired. The FYD belief is that people must be accepted and respected no matter what communication

Initiative Training with FYD-NZ (courtesy of Chris Blum)

they use – NZSL, or oral, or Signed English or a mixture. This belief is a bridge to understanding, so that people can be united, not separated by different communication systems. When parents, hearing friends and Deaf people see for themselves that deaf and hearing people can get on well together, then they believe it.

(p200, Talking Hands, Listening Eyes)

Damian and Sue returned to the UK in 1998 and Jennifer Brain was appointed as CEO of NZAD. This impacted on the size of the FYD-NZ team and left Chris Blum trying to manage the programme on his own, with the support of volunteers. Despite this, 1998 was a successful year; attendance at training and children's camps was good. 1999 was a quieter year with a loss of momentum. Although it was recognised that FYD-NZ was offering much to Deaf people, it was a difficult area to fund.

FYD-NZ was discontinued in 2001, due to the lack of funding. However, we know that by 2007 at least, the FYD legacy continued to live on through the development of youth groups such as the Auckland DEAFinitely Youth Group, the Wellington and Christchurch Youth Groups, Deaf Youth Aotearoa and Magnet.[4]

We asked Chris to sum up what had made him do the things he did:

Some people accept barriers
    Some people get frustrated and want to change things.

(Chris Blum)

---

4   Dugdale, P. in *Talking Hands, Listening Eyes*, pp213-217

Embassies (1993-2000)

In 1993, the regional offices of FYD became known as 'Embassies', drawing reference from the diplomatic in that Ambassadors are based in Embassies. In line with our ratio policy, these offices were to be staffed by three deaf and one hearing person.

Our model for the Embassies was that they were to support the work of at least four volunteer Ambassadors; young people who had come through the four year NTP and were considered qualified, through experience and knowledge, to represent FYD in their local regions and to take responsibility for local FYD activities – projects, deaf awareness and initiative training. They also served as resource centres for youth workers to help them in supporting young deaf people and involving them in their programmes.

Our first Embassy; the London and South East in East Grinstead, was officially opened on 1st October 1993 followed by two others in Newcastle and Birmingham. We had approximately 15 Ambassadors linked to the Embassies supporting about 45 to 90 participants per year and taking responsibility for 3 to 6 regional projects, 6-9 regional Initiative days, 2 initiative weekends and up to 9 deaf awareness days.

The North East Embassy had been established on the back of some very hard working and motivated volunteers and fundraisers who helped us to make the fist tentative footholds in earlier years.

> One of the funniest moments must be NEAT's[5] fund-raising pub collection – we visited all the pubs in Middlesbrough on a busy Friday night dressed in the opposite sex's nightwear and raised a few hundred pounds for local FYD Projects (a lot of money in those days). Although the FYD Management Team weren't entirely sure of this exercise following FYD principles, the team spirit was incredible and taking money off merry revelers was so easy, especially if we girls gave the blokes a peck on the cheek!
>
> (Claire Ingham)

Terry Thompson was the main lead on the Embassy concept, which created staff manuals and supported the establishment of local support groups to help the teams. He was supported by Claire to lead the development and delivery of our national project work and Damian became responsible for the training and managing of the Embassy workers after Terry had initially set things up.

By the end of 1993, we were ready to open a fourth Embassy in Wales and the emerging work in New Zealand and Australia was giving rise to the consideration for potentially opening overseas Embassies. We looked ahead 3 to 4 years and to also the possibility of opening up in Liverpool, the South West and Northern Ireland. We were also exploring ideas for opening a European Embassy and a conference to launch the International Training Centre.

---

5   North East Action Team

I was appointed as Development Office for Wales and based at an office in PHAB Wales in Penarth Road, Cardiff. Initially I started the job without an administrator. My line manager was Evelyn Carter. Together we interviewed candidates and eventually appointed Rachael Edwards. She was easy to lip-read and she learnt British Sign Language and took to it like a duck to the water. She was very efficient and a great source of support.

From there we organised training and projects from our office. At the beginning I was new to managing and thus when I had my supervision meetings with Evelyn she started to empower me to think for myself. This was known as throwing the ball back in my court.

I developed through the job and I went to the Birmingham office based at Ladywood Leisure Centre with the other Development Officers namely Keith Wardle (later Wardle-Peck), John Walker and Katie Clarke.

One of the biggest challenges and it remains the same now. The mindset and pace is different from England. It was easier to recruit for projects and training in the South Wales compared to the North. Probably because in the North they were more political focused.

(Stuart Parkinson)

In January 1994, Mandy Crump was studying up in the north-west at Chester College. She had been invited by Evelyn to join her on an FYD business visit to Germany. However, Mandy had to decline because it clashed with her finals. Instead, she tabled a proposition for Evelyn to consider. Chester College had supported Mandy's work at Bude through their Student Enterprise development programme and so, in return for the support; she suggested that the NTP should develop links with the college to consolidate their own enterprise schemes. Mandy suggested basing a North West Embassy at the college, which would also serve to make the college more accessible to disabled students. The college was also very interested in developing international links and was organising an international conference to which it wished to invite Damian and Terry.

In January, John Walker was appointed Embassy Officer in Scotland, but the Wales Embassy was experiencing some difficulties due to the lack of volunteering resources. As it turned out, there were also delays in the development of the Scotland Embassy, the siting of the office was under review but things were looking encouraging because we had delivered three projects. I was surprised that my fellow countrymen were not picking up the opportunities as quickly as I was expecting, but I remained confident that the initial problems would be overcome when young people saw the development of our work, through the training programme and the sports festival.

By the end of the summer, John had relocated back to London/SE and we were advertising the Scotland post. All our Embassy staff members were under increasing pressure with their workloads, so we extended their training in the 'Staff

College' for an extra year to allow them more time to get qualifications.

With FYD coming under financial pressure, we directed the training programme to produce quality rather than quantity and tasked the Embassy workers to take the lead in building a network of volunteers, on the FYD NTP, and to produce a higher proportion of Ambassadors to meet our future needs. All this was to be done on top of their workload supporting young people and helping them to integrate into their local communities.

Embassy staffing costs were going over budget because we were employing agency staff in some regions to cover unfilled administration support vacancies. The consequences of this were a cut back on PR development and fundraising posts and a hold on plans for international expansion. We also put plans in place for the sustainability of the senior management team as Evelyn, Terry and myself were all approaching retirement age.

The Directors had been reviewing the Wales Embassy and we made the decision to close Wales down at the end of August 1995 for the following reasons:

a)   Pressures on the FYD budget
b)   Need for consolidation focusing on England with a programme in Wales supported by Birmingham as this arrangement was working well with Scotland supported by the Newcastle Embassy.

When the funds from the Welsh Office ran out in 1995 I was sadly made redundant but looking back it was the best job that I ever did without question and I made so many friends and have so many memories.

(Stuart Parkinson)

This was perhaps one of the saddest moments of my FYD career. Terry and I sat with Stuart and explained the situation and offered to discuss possible future career development options with him, work that would be available outside of FYD. This decision had an impact on morale and reactions from people in Wales. We continued to have a presence there, through a series of training workshops that built up a network of volunteers to support the projects. Meanwhile, three other Embassy staff enrolled at their local colleges for NVQ level 3 Supervisory Management and also enrolled for the Institute of Personnel & Development Certificate, to become qualified trainers at NVQ level 3.

Despite this setback, we did have positive news about the success of the Embassies in the recruitment of participants and in expanding our network. They built up the number of participants on our projects by 56% in 1994/5 and we were expecting another large increase for 1995/6. Our next task was getting project participants to move onto the NTP to become future supervisors and leaders.

At the Directors meeting in December 1995 the challenges of maintaining Embassies in Scotland and Wales were attributed to three main problems; finance,

Embassy Staff c1998: Naomi Guest (London), Jane Higgins (North West), Marcel Hirshman (South East), Helen Thew (North East), Wendy Callaghan (South West), John Walker, Keith Wardle-Peck (Midlands) Mandy Crump (ACD Manager) (FYD)

employing experienced staff and the 'national' difficulty (experienced by most organisations) in trying to run Welsh and Scottish activities from what is seen as an "English" organisation. In his departing report, Terry drew up a very comprehensive review of our current position as to what we might develop in respect of Scotland and Wales. He suggested that we could develop a franchise arrangement so that each country had their own subsidiary company, with their own responsibilities, except for overall support from Evelyn and myself. Although staff and volunteers would be able to benefit from the NTP in England, the local Embassy programmes would not involve English management or support. He suggested that Wales could be restarted in October 1996 with a Welsh Lottery Grant and for Scotland to start in 1998 with similar funding.

We never re-opened in Wales and Scotland but instead, by the beginning of 1999, we were operating through a fifth Embassy in the South West. Our Embassy Development team was comprised of Jane Higgins in Chester, Jannine Williams and Helen Thew job-sharing in Newcastle, Sharon Gamblin (now Smith) in Nuneaton, Wendy Callaghan in Taunton and Marcel Hirshman at East Grinstead. They were all carrying out important work within their local communities, encouraging young people to take part in a variety of FYD projects and training opportunities and we were all very grateful to the volunteers who supported our work locally, either as project leaders, supervisors, communicators or community fundraisers. This was all duly recognised when we won the Guardian Jerwood Award for our Community work.

Marcel Hirshman and Pauline Collishaw were both featured in the East Grinstead Courier[6] under the headline *"Confidence Despite Deafness"* where they explained their roles as Embassy Development Officer and Administrator:

> We work together in a partnership with the aim of giving deaf people confidence to work and play in society because as a deaf child you can be bullied and excluded. Many deaf children are born to hearing parents and do not have much contact with other deaf people. It is surprising how many deaf children think they are the only ones in the world who cannot hear.

Marcel put forward a commonly held view that Sign Language should be taught in schools as an option:

> People do not recognise us as a minority group. We have our own language which is different from English so we are a language minority group.

In September 2000, Evelyn retired and Mark Perry was appointed as the new Executive Director. Funding difficulties forced us to close the Newcastle office for one year on the 7th April 2000. Right from the outset of this decision, there was campaigning from local volunteers and participants who wanted to see the office re-opened. Coincidentally, at the end of that summer our newly appointed South West replacement Embassy Development Officer resigned and so on balance we felt that the funds allocated there would be better used to reopen in Newcastle.

Mark was in the process of carrying out a review of FYD's position overall and he began a period of interviewing all the staff individually and in teams to give them an opportunity to contribute. Sharon resigned from the Embassy in Nuneaton and we covered her role, temporarily, subject to the review findings.

---

6   *East Grinstead Courier*, April 8th 1999.

7

The Merger

To make sense of what happened, we need to step back a few years before the merger to examine the issues that were behind the decision to open a dialogue with the National Deaf Children's Society.

The Trustees designated 1995 'A Year of Consolidation' to avoid the perennial cash flow crisis that was becoming more frequent. We sought to maintain a tight expenditure, whilst working to increase income in the first half of the year and so, therefore, increase our reserves. But early on we realised our community fundraising just wasn't hitting it. This we blamed on the National Lottery. People just weren't giving.

In the first two decades of FYD (1970s – 1980s), we held regular door-to-door and street collections. One of these activities was held under the auspices of the 'Alexander Rose Day'. This income was important to the Trust because, obviously, it was unrestricted and allowed us to use the funds in whatever way we felt necessary within charity law. For the most part, our collections contributed towards 'core costs' (office administration, finance, fundraising, public relations, rent / rates).

Just before the introduction of the National Lottery Bill, most charities estimated that they would lose up to a third of their income and FYD was no exception. Once the Lottery had been introduced by the Department of Culture Media and Sport in November 1994, the general public gradually began to stop making cash donations to charities and started buying lottery tickets instead. In effect, the Lottery took money away from charities and then began to control how it would all be spent and who was going to receive the funds. For example, in the very first call for bids, charities had to align their applications to the alleviation of 'poverty'. Many commentators saw this as a move to get charities to solve problems that perhaps should be otherwise the responsibility of government.

One impending casualty was the National Council for Voluntary Youth Services, which was facing closure. As a member organisation, FYD responded to their request for a support grant of £100 to assist them through their crisis. To mitigate any forthcoming problems, we were also making preparations the formation of a new charitable Company limited by guarantee.

Once again, we used our own reserves to cover our deficit for the 1994/5 financial year and our focus on *consolidation* was aimed at avoiding any unnecessary spending to enable us to build up our reserves once more. At the summer board meeting we faced the challenge of having to make severe cuts; consequently we cut back on staff training, public relations and reduced the number of administration trainees at East Grinstead.

Evelyn and I both agreed that we would both scale down our working hours as Director and Co-Director, if it became necessary, to make savings. I made it clear that I was also prepared to reduce my working hours to four days a week from July and job-share from January 1996. Now that FYD was also a limited company, there was the option of taking out bank overdrafts to manage any future cash flow difficulties, but only on the condition that we were confident that funds would be coming in to cover these commitments. .

For our house-to-house collections, we had agreements with an agency for 22 collections. We were also chasing up a large private donation, which had been pledged in writing, but had yet to be presented.

We also debated again the option of raising money by selling our expertise to other organisations in the form of specialised training. Other issues we considered were how staff could be released from their normal work without impacting on performance. VAT would have to be paid and running costs incurred before we saw any income benefits. We asked Damian to carry out some research and report back in January 1996.

Interestingly, after completing his feasibility study Damian recommended to the Board that we should not sell FYD training skills and expertise to other organisations because:

a) There were no members of staff available to take on the job – everyone was already working to tight remits

b) The income generated would not be cost effective – it would be easier to raise money through our normal methods.

c) VAT registration would affect course fees and any increase in fees could dampen recruitment

d) Offering the service could trigger excessive demands and we would not be in a position to effectively deliver in a timely manner and;

e) There was still a lack of skills amongst existing staff to actually deliver was proposed

But we didn't entirely rule this option out, because fundraising was becoming more competitive and we needed to be sustainable.

The use of emails and video as a means of communication and training was very much in its infancy and I suggested that our training programme could take advantage of this. We could use email for networking and use video as a training aid. However I was met with some concerns with regards to using video as there was a need to have some interaction for development purposes, but nevertheless, we asked our staff to investigate further.

By the end of August, our income and expenditure levels were better than our estimates, thanks to some diligent work by all staff. Monthly fundraising targets were being met from Trust and Companies and some community fundraising was also helping. But we still had three areas of concern:

1. We were heavily dependent on the National Lottery and two other large applications to meet our requirements for the year, but would not know the outcome until October/November.
2. The House-to-House collections had made a good start but it was too early in the year to know if we would hit our target. Plus the private donation had failed to appear and so we decided to discount it.
3. Our conservative estimates expected an income shortfall of about 6% that would still give us a small end of year surplus. We were unable to guarantee cash flows as we remained in the hands of those who sent in donations, but we felt that the cuts we had made earlier in the year would see us over the finish line.

But we were not out of the woods, our Honourary Treasurer had moved overseas and we needed to find a replacement. To add to our affairs, Terry Thompson had submitted his resignation to take effect from 31st December. There was no connection between Terry's decision and the departure of our Honourary Treasurer; it was coincidental but difficult none the less.

By October, the expected grant decisions had been delayed until November and we had to take out bank overdrafts, which put staffing at risk if the grants did not materialise. In place we had plans not to reduce project delivery, but to look at back office functions and put on hold any staffing replacements, planned staff meetings and cancel the Christmas mail out. We were also faced with the possibility of implementing staff redundancies but felt that we could avoid this by reducing top salaries.

At our Christmas milestone, we were pleased that all our efforts to consolidate brought our spending to within 0.4% of the budget and our income generation was 0.8% better than forecasted. But we still had problems. The house-to house collections were not doing well and the manager we had appointed had resigned due to ill health. Our earlier house-to-house expectations were now considered to have been very optimistic and although we were on target in the first seven months, the next five were not under control. Some collections had been cancelled and others had been moved without any reporting to Terry. Our supervision had failed to detect these problems earlier.

After Christmas, the results of our house-to house activity showed that we had only managed to collect 50% of the target and costs for collections were running at 46% of income! Despite the high cost, we decided to continue with collections into the new financial year because the income we created was making a significant contribution to our unrestricted income and reserves. To fill the void left by the recently departed manager, we sent Pauline Collishaw on a training course so that she could manage this activity and monitor the performances of the agencies.

We took the opportunity to be the beneficiary of BBC radio's *"This Week's Good Cause"* to raise enough funds to balance books by the financial year-end. I don't think people realised how demanding these opportunities are. We needed to secure a celebrity; pay BBC fees, supply volunteers to go to Ealing to help take telephone pledges and we had to provide them with a script. All this had to be presented two weeks before recording, which was all to be completed two weeks before broadcasting in April! We eventually secured the support of Angela Rippon to present our appeal.

Despite our very best efforts at consolidation, things were still very tight; we could not afford to courier boxes of the *Signpost* newsletter out to our Embassies, so we had to ask staff to transport them in their cars or on public transport during their work trips. We even looked at the amount of coloured paper being used by the various offices as this was costing twice the price of white.

The following year was also relentless. We closed down the house-to-house collections knowing that we were losing unrestricted income. When making grant applications we had to start building in an allowance for overheads etc. We were conscious that this would not cover the situation in its entirety and that we were too heavily dependent on project income. There was no question that we needed a senior full time fundraiser. There was however a question of status. Should the post holder have equal status with the co-Directors and how would we incorporate the philosophy of FYD into the FR strategy?

I agreed to take responsibility for bringing in funds and was set a target of £74,000 to meet our budget and reserves, By December 1996, I had managed to raise £53,000. This was complemented by a fundraising highlight in 1996; a Sign Singing Roadshow covering ten days in November where Damian, Keith Wardle and Charles Butler toured England raising much needed funds and generating a whole host of new contacts and new recruits for the training programme.

Our Christmas Sign Singing events brought in many new faces and delivered inspiration to others. I was pleased that we had achieved our budget for the financial year, but I was determined to continue into the spring and maintain momentum. Again I want to re-acknowledge the team who were at East Grinstead that year, for giving me their support – and the Directors for their faith in our capabilities. I reviewed the year feeling encouraged to know that teams really do work. *A team is a group of individuals coming together to achieve a goal, task or objective.* Truly, the last few months of 1996 saw this for real and it was a pleasure to be part of that. We closed the last few months of that year with a new Chair of Trustees and an Honorary Company Secretary. I also gave notice to retire at the end of July 1998.

Six years later, the impact of the National Lottery was reviewed at a government

Fundraising Roadshow November 1996 (FYD)

Sub Committee of the Department of Culture, Media and Sport:[1]

An unfortunate side-effect of the introduction of the National Lottery was that the self-funding capabilities of the not-for-profit sector in the UK were significantly damaged, as revenues fell. Although the National Lottery is generous in its funding of a number of charities, this funding is distributed on a 'project by project' basis, and does not constitute a reliable source of core funding. The Community Fund, responsible for distributing National Lottery money to charities has an unofficial policy of limiting funding to six year periods. As a result, many charities have found that funding has been withdrawn at crucial times and have been left without the necessary income to continue with their most basic work.

Although I had reached my official retirement age in 1998, I continued to work voluntarily in a new role as FYD President alongside Evelyn and at the end of 1999, I went back to work voluntarily in the SE Embassy office to support the administrator and Ethnic Minorities worker in the absence of our Embassy Development Officer. Our ethnic minorities work was based in London and funded by Bridgehouse Estates. But by 2000 we could not longer secure funds to maintain this important

---

1   Select Committee on Culture, Media and Sport Memoranda, Submission 3, 3rd May 2002. *The problems for Charities, Introduction of the National Lottery—effects on UK charities*

work and in addition, we had to stop delivering our iconic Crystal Palace Sports Festival.

The National Lottery affected the entire voluntary sector and it saw greater demands placed on Charitable Trusts and corporations to support our work. But their resources were also dwindling too and they had many more organisations demanding their support. Which, in turn, forced them to drastically change their approach in respect of whom they decided to fund and by how much.[2]

As we started the first financial year of the new millennium, our Honourary Treasurer wrote a paper titled *Year of Challenge 2000 -2001*. He did this to try and focus the trustees' minds to the fact that 70% of our income was grant funded and that this created disadvantages for us as the grant market was more competitive and our loyal grant makers were looking for 'new' things to fund.

The report highlighted the same issues and made similar recommendations to those raised in the *Consolidation* report five years earlier. The situation was still the same; we had long term commitments to staff and premises but only short term funding; there was no flexibility in the most efficient deployment of staff and the management of several small grants from different donors was time consuming to manage, report on and justify. We were still chasing deficits and expenditure reductions. The recommendations were; to avoid end of year pressures by securing 75% of known funds in place at the start of each financial year; look for costs savings in overheads; implement an unrestricted income strategy and try to secure larger grants to cover projects rather than trying to manage several small ones. The challenge was selecting the ideas that would generate the best return and deciding how far FYD should change its activities to meet the changing priorities of grant makers.

Neither the staff nor trustees wanted to discuss or commit to the recommendations in the *Year of Challenge* report until a new Executive Director had been appointed. We soldiered on, committing to unavoidable expenditures such as the new stakeholder pension scheme and fundraising through another TV appeal and Gift Aid. We started to build a website and continued with community fundraising through marathons, penny-back shopping and sign singing. We also recognised that in the regional offices, we were trying to maintain staff morale in the face of employing unskilled staff, due to lower salary levels, and delaying the implementation of cost of living salary increases.

We didn't recognise anything as being a quick fix solution, as low-cost entry schemes would take time to develop a return; legacies for example, required a four-year cycle of activity to gain returns on investment. We were also reliant on our Embassy staff to create local and regional sources of income. There were questions from our fundraising staff about whether we had the right people in the regions, to make the funding approaches, and were we able to give them the managerial support to be successful.

---

2   See Chapter 5 (Prince's Trust)

Mark Perry accepted the post of Executive Director in the summer of 2000 and immediately began liaising with Evelyn and the staff on an unpaid basis until he was due to start full-time in September. At his first Board meeting, it was made very clear to him that we were facing a deficit of £100,000 at the mid-point of the year. Decisions were made not to fill any new vacancies except to provide temporary cover if essential. Prior to Mark's appointment a new Head of Fundraising had already been appointed to work on a full-time salary for four days a week. Damian was promoted to Director of Operations and Development as part of the new leadership team. Even taking this into account, it was acknowledged that FYD salaries were not competitive enough to attract good staff and that the Board needed to focus on sorting out the leadership team as a first step. The September Board meeting was also the last in Evelyn's very long journey with FYD.

> In conclusion, I would like to pay tribute to all FYD staff who continued to work hard and stayed committed, often in the face of adversity. I know they feel sometimes that they are not always recognised for what has been achieved, but often criticised for what has not been achieved.
> It would be good to remember that there are many thousands of young deaf people and their families who have benefitted from their efforts – this work is important, even at the most basic level.
>
> (Evelyn Carter, 28th June 2000)

By November, Mark had carried out his Structural Review of FYD by meeting the trustees and all the staff both individually and in groups/teams in order to make sense of what was required. At the end of November the deficit had been reduced to £60,000 and further staff vacancies (created by resignations) gave him an opportunity to restructure staff teams. Mark's plan was to downgrade income targets, create new projects for funding, consolidate both reserves and overheads and operate from only two offices (East Grinstead and Nuneaton). These changes meant the closure of the other Embassies leading to staff redundancies but they were balanced with some redeployment to other posts at the Nuneaton office. In spite of the financial difficulties, Mark wanted to invest in growth and increase salaries in order that the remaining staff would be motivated and retained and essential new posts could be filled. The impact was to reduce the staff team from 21 employees to 16 employees with the same overall salary costs. FYD also had difficulty finding a good management accountant who would be committed to us, and who would diligently prepare our management accounts – crucial to the well-being of any organisation.

There were also external changes beyond our control. For over two decades, we had built up an excellent relationship with the Department for Education and Employment. But our main contact there announced that they were stepping down and the work would be passed on to the new ConneXions Unit in Sheffield –

Damian Barry in action (FYD)

this required new relationships to be built and a new momentum and confidence in our work to be established. I agreed to continue encouraging the South East network of contacts to stay involved with FYD I also joined the PR Working Group with Mark and the fundraising manager. We were aiming to build up three months worth of working capital.

In the final quarter of 2000/1, our deficit was £95,000 with £61,000 in reserves. Implementing the new SORP[3] accounting system under Charity Commission guidelines, meant that there was much less leeway than before. Mark's Structural Review plans were also scaled down due to the worsening financial situation and instead of advertising for three new managers to head the projects, two managers were taken on through temporary contracts. We were also going to ask people to pay increased fees for their training; we knew this was a risky departure from our normal approach via subsidies. But there was a very real threat of FYD being insolvent by July 2001 and we were bracing ourselves to make further redundancies if income did not materialise.

FYD was nothing without its projects so it was working hard with three large funders; the Camelot Foundation to fund the family intervention work for three years; the Home Office to fund a volunteering Officer and BBC Children in Need for our Summer programme. Contingencies were also in place if these funding

3   Statements of Recommended Practice

applications were to fail. In comparison to March 2000, when FYD employed 26 staff, it was now operating with just 15, many in short-term or seconded posts.

On 23rd February, Damian informed Mark that he was leaving at Easter to join the Red Cross and it was likely that Sue would follow at the end of May. This presented Mark with an opportunity to run FYD with a flatter Management Team by splitting Damian's post – Director of Operations and Development to Head of Development and upgrading the Training Manager post to Head of Training. We appointed Stuart Harrison to Head of Community Development. In the conclusion of his final report to the trustees on the 24th March Damian's parting words were:

> It has been a pleasure to be involved in FYD using the passion invoked by Denis Uttley to encourage positive change between deaf and hearing people. Good luck for the future and hopefully, one day, Northern Ireland will benefit from what FYD has to offer.

Damian and Sue have kept true to their word and went onto build successful careers in Northern Ireland and elsewhere. Implementing their extensive FYD experience they have established a very successful training and mentoring programme there.

Financial Year 2001/2002

After the initial work by Damian in building a great relationship with the Camelot Foundation, Mark and Stuart worked with Alistair Wright to build upon this and secure income for the Early Intervention & Family work (£557k). Mark also worked with the new Head of Training, Sally McMahon, to bring in £285k to the Training programme from ConneXions. Despite these successes, the Trustees recognised that insufficient unrestricted income was being generated. The future was beginning to look problematic. Indeed, by February 2002 FYD was in a desperate situation. With FYD unable to guarantee that the deficit for 2001/2 was going to be cleared, the Finance Advisory Group, a subsidiary of the Trustees, asked Mark to develop a Contingency Plan with the following elements:

- Cease trading
- Close Head Office and relocate
- Seek a merger partner

FYD Board Meeting 23rd February 2002

Following previous weeks of communications backwards and forwards between the Trustees and Mark, nobody was satisfied that they had any concrete solutions to the current operating model. Mark then made a recommendation to the Trustees to shut down operations at East Grinstead and establish Nuneaton as the single operating base for all FYD activities. The impact was to announce another wave of redundancies at East Court Mansion (5 staff) with the Executive Director and Head of Community Development transferring to Nuneaton.

The day we actually closed the East Grinstead offices was for me a very emotional and personal experience. I kept thinking about all the work we had done there over the years and all the wonderful people who had come and gone. We had to sort through unnecessary furniture and paperwork and dispose of it in large skips and shred hundreds of documents. I remember Stuart, who was not in the best of health; helping to carry heavy loads down the narrow awkward staircases. Hamish and I were just so sad for everyone.

At this stage, there appeared to be a possible reprieve from a merger with Deafax, but this needed Deafax Board approval. When it became known that Deafax was not going to be an option. The Trustees met briefly at some time in late February/early March to discuss the implications of the move with Deafax not going through and the option of approaching the NDCS was discussed. The NDCS were considered to be a very good strategic fit and it was agreed that the FYD Treasurer and Chair would open up discussions with them.

Incidentally, Susan Daniels, Chief Executive of the NDCS was certainly aware of the challenges that FYD was facing and that it was continuing to navigate a tough path and was looking at options that included the search for a merger partner. At some point after the trustees meeting, there was an exchange of text messages between Susan and Mark in which they both agreed to start initial discussions on the potential of merging. The FYD Treasurer went over to the NDCS offices to meet Susan and her senior staff. Things were starting to move very quickly with the NDCS and the trustees were called back for another meeting.

FYD Board Meeting 27th March 2002

When they met, the trustees had two options available to them. Firstly, discussions with the NDCS had proved so far to be productive and their formal offer was to carry out a period of due diligence with the view to a merger[4]. Secondly, another option was put forward at the eleventh hour by one of the trustees was to work with the Enabling Foundation.

It came down to a majority decision that it was not feasible to be involved in two simultaneous due diligence processes because we did not have the resources to cope with that[5] and it was always felt by most of those present that the family intervention programmes and children's activities of FYD and NDCS would have a natural overlap. Furthermore, the recent Camelot Foundation award to fund a major family programme would be attractive to the NDCS.

Throughout April and May, the NDCS were generous with their time and support in two ways: firstly they provided a small amount of funding support to FYD activity and secondly, they guided FYD through the due diligence process, having

---

4   Items 9.10, 9.12 FYD Board Minutes 31/5/02
5   item 9.11 FYD Board Minutes 31/5/02

taken control of this following FYD trustee approval to merge with the NDCS.

FYD Board Meeting 31st May 2002

Susan Daniels and Mark Astarita came to this meeting to discuss the outcome of the due diligence undertaken so far. The process had confirmed that a merger would be of great benefit to both organisations. There was very little overlap in each others work except for the family early interventions and the merger would *give no financial benefit to NDCS; rather the benefit is purely from the synergy of the respective missions.*[6]

Once Susan and Mark had left the meeting, the Trustees regrouped to discuss their options. The majority (with the exception of one) agreed to go ahead and transfer control of FYD to interim trustees to be appointed by the NDCS.

This decision was made on the grounds that FYD was facing insolvency and therefore had two options a) liquidation or b) a merger. A core team of project staff would also be safeguarded by the merger and transferred to the NDCS. Unfortunately, despite his efforts to save FYD, Mark Perry himself had to accept redundancy along with other members of the support staff whose jobs were not covered by project funding.

5th June 2002

Mark Astarita and Lucy Jago visited the Nuneaton offices to inform the FYD staff officially about the merger and what was going to happen next. Once this had been done, press releases were sent out. This followed prior correspondence with key funders (including Camelot Foundation and ConneXions) to keep them on board.

1st November 2002

After a period of further work and discussions with principal funders a full merger transferring the assets and liabilities of FYD into NDCS took place. FYD continued as a dormant company. It's core work continued with a successful mix of arts and sports activities, personal development training programmes for young deaf people and an early intervention programme for families with deaf children.

Unfortunately FYD was not able to manage the challenge of building sufficient unrestricted funds, since the introduction of the National Lottery. Whilst I am deeply sad that FYD are not able to help today and tomorrow's generation aside from the activities through NDCS, which continue to flourish, I believe that the 40-year FYD project was a huge success. We invested time, energy and money to work with young deaf people and their hearing peers over the decades. The young deaf people who graduated through FYD remain a huge inspiration and we are fortunate to continue to benefit from the leadership legacy, even today.

---

6   Item 9.6 FYD Board Minutes 31/5/02

8

The Legacy of FYD

H aving to merge with the NDCS doesn't mean that FYD was a failure – far from that. It was one of the most successful youth development programmes of the 1960s – 1990s because it has left an extremely strong and vibrant LEGACY of deaf and hearing people, who had been given the opportunity to lead at many different levels in the organisation and used that experience as their personal their stepping-stone to greater things. FYD's former participants are today demanding that opportunities to lead be created so that deaf children of the future can benefit from the FYD legacy:

> I remember like being part of a family and how we all gelled together and this remains with me today, being a believer that sign language users or people who understand deafness can all be part of a community, working and socialising together and not just deaf people.
>
> (Reg Cobb, CEO Gloucestershire Deaf Association.)

> I remember one training session I was in charge of a group as part of the training, we had to achieve something like make a plan to build a bridge or something. We as a group ran out of time but the trainer was pleased at how I managed the people in the group so in spite of 'failing' I was pleased at how I got the group to work together and have the space for each individual to fully contribute to the task, which is how I run my workshops today.
>
> (Caroline Parker MBE, Actress/Entertainer)

> Morag Rosie's dreams of creating a world where deaf and hearing can work together and that communication would not become a hindrance to a friendship. This dream is something that I continue to hold dear to life and try to adhere to in breaking down barriers which can stop friendships.
>
> (Fleur Leslie, BSL/English Interpreter)

> The legacy of FYD's work over 40 years was so strong – it transformed the leadership qualities of so many deaf professionals and advocates working in the UK and abroad… at a time when equality and diversity was started to be

recognised and taken seriously in the workplace.

(Mark Perry)

It goes without saying that FYD left behind a legacy in which deaf and hearing participants have profited from its outcomes and a good number have made noteworthy contributions to the wider social good of society. The challenge is to empirically describe what that impact has been.

To start off with, I do want everyone to bear in mind that not everyone who came through the programme became a project leader or a member of our staff. Whilst the initial reason for establishing a leadership programme was to find volunteers to run our programmes, not everyone came on board and there will be many reasons for that. Preston Bottger, who, amongst many who have studied and researched the concept of leadership said that the process of becoming a 'leader', in the sense of taking on responsibilities as a project volunteer, or a member of staff, comes down to how much responsibility an individual is prepared to take on at any particular moment in time. Bottger[1] said that it depends on what level of leadership people want to aspire to because the higher you go, the tasks become *'Massive, complex and conflictual. The playing field and boundaries become less certain'.*

Not everyone is either prepared to take on tasks or has the confidence or experience at the time to do so. Our aim certainly was to try and help as many young people as we could to develop enough experience to give them the confidence that they needed to move on in life. For some this comes quickly and for others they need more time; this will always be the case. Through our work at FYD, we were realising the aspiration of Denis Uttley to provide young deaf people with the experience and skills to enable them to make a positive transition into adulthood. Empowering them to make decisions about training and education and to make them attractive to employers. It was about creating empowered, resilient young deaf people.

To be able to measure the impact of FYD as a youth organisation, I am going to refer very briefly to some tools that were not available to us when FYD was in operation. FYD was about supporting the development of young people's social and emotional capabilities by intervening as early as possible through our participation programme. As an active member of the youth sector in the UK, FYD was challenged by sponsors, charitable trusts and the government to provide quantitative evidence of the difference that it was making and to articulate the value that we brought to young people and wider society. In the beginning, the evidence base for the significance of social and emotional capabilities was elusive because we could not agree, amongst ourselves in the youth sector, on a consensus around language and definitions and it was considered difficult to measure or evidence the development of these capabilities.

In the summer of 2012, 12 years after FYD had merged with the NDCS, the

---

1   *Preston Bottger is Professor of Leadership and General Management at IMD.*

Catalyst consortium[2] worked with the Department for Education (DfE) as a strategic partner on the DfE Transition programme. They created a framework to enable service providers and local commissioners to articulate and demonstrate impact in improving outcomes for young people.

A Framework of Outcomes for Young People was published in July 2012 but practitioners in the youth sector found the concepts and practice confusing. So, after further consultations, the framework was re-published in December 2014 as a guideline document with worked examples. The essence of the framework is that:

- There is substantial and growing evidence that developing social and emotional capabilities supports the achievement of positive life outcomes, including educational attainment, employment and health.
- Supporting the development of young people's underlying social and emotional capabilities is a strong theme in the current governments Positive for Youth strategy, which encourages a stronger focus on early support to help all young people succeed.
- The framework proposes a model of seven interlinked clusters of social and emotional capabilities that are of value to all young people, supported by a strong evidence base, demonstrating their link to positive life outcomes.
- It also provides a matrix of tools to measure these capabilities, outlining which capabilities each tool covers, and key criteria that might be considered in selecting an appropriate tool.

The UK government's Positive for Youth[3] strategy states that the process of personal and social development includes:

Developing social, communication and team working skills; the ability to learn from experience, control behaviours and make good choices; and the self-esteem, resilience, and motivation to persists towards goals and overcome setbacks.

Catalyst recognised that the process of social and personal development is often through the provision of developmental educational opportunities: space for young people to actively learn, to participate, and to take responsibility. The 2008 National Occupational Standards for Youth Work stated that:

The key focus of youth work is to enable young people to develop holistically, working with them to facilitate their personal, social and educational

---

2   Catalyst was led by the National Council for Voluntary Youth Services and supported by the National Youth Agency, Social Enterprise Coalition and The Young Foundation. It operated from 2011-2013.
3   DfE (2011) Positive for Youth: a new approach to cross-government policy to young people aged 13-19

development, to enable them to develop their voice, influence and place in society, and to reach their full potential.

Table 2 below lists the seven clusters of social and emotional capabilities identified in the Framework.

Table 2	
Clusters	**Social & Emotional capabilities**
Communication	Explaining; expressing; presenting; listening; questioning; using different ways of communicating.
Confidence & Agency	Self-reliance; self-esteem; self-efficacy; self-belief; ability to shape your own life and the world around you.
Creativity	Imagining alternative ways of doing things; applying learning in new contexts; enterprising; innovating; remaining open to new ideas.
Managing Feelings	Reviewing; self-awareness; reflecting; self-regulating; self-accepting.
Planning & problem solving	Navigating resources; organising; setting & achieving goals; decision-making; researching; analysing; critical thinking; questioning & challenging; evaluating risks; reliability.
Relationships & Leadership	Motivating others; valuing and contributing to team working; negotiating; establishing positive relationships; interpreting others; managing conflict; empathising.
Resilience & Determination	Self-disciplined; self-management; self-motivated; concentrating; having a sense of purpose; persistent; self-controlled.

Catalyst argued that these clusters have a significant impact on the public purse by providing the following benefits to society because young people would:

- Have less need for health services
- Contribute to the economy through labour market participation
- Be less dependent on welfare
- Be less likely be subject to the criminal justice system
- Be part of a strengthened community through leadership and democratic participation.

After the Framework was published, the Behavioral Insights Team, a company owned by the Cabinet Office of the UK government refined the seven outcomes in Table 2 and defined six intrinsic qualities in young people which can be developed through high quality youth interventions that are strongly linked to hard extrinsic outcomes such as employability (Table 3):

Table 3	
Intrinsic Qualities	**Definition**
Empathy	The ability to understand and share the feelings of another
Problem Solving	The ability to reason, use available information and think laterally in order to reach a goal or end point
Cooperation	Working together with others to the same end or goal
Grit and resilience	Grit is the tendency to sustain interest in and effort toward very long-term goals. Resilience is the ability to bounce back.
Sense of community	Identification as part of a community, perception of agency within it and propensity to take prosocial action
Educational attitudes	Understanding of the value of education and taking an interest in building knowledge and skills.

When researching for this book, we invited former participants of the FYD programme to share their testimonials with us. What I want to do now is to take the six intrinsic qualities from Table 3 and demonstrate the positive life outcomes of those who participated in FYD's social action.

Empathy: The ability to understand and share the feelings of another

Probably the core quality that we developed in young people through the *'friendship insurance'* envisioned by Denis Uttley was enabling both deaf and hearing people to understand and empathise with each other's feelings. For young deaf people in many mainstreaming activities, this seldom manifests itself, unless a non-deaf person takes the initiative to help their deaf peers. Far too often, mainstreaming of deaf and disabled young people is left to chance and indifference often ensues. Despite over 40 years of mainstreaming education, research continues to confirm that for the majority of deaf and hard of hearing young people, a lack of appropriate communication and social support is undermining confidence and creates social isolation, leaving as many as 60% of young deaf people vulnerable to bullying.[4]

I am raising my glass. FYD opened up my world at that time. I was a product of mainstream education; I was struggling with my identity, not fitting in anywhere. Went on a leadership course with Craig Crowley leading. I find it very hard appropriately express my gratitude for that weekend; it changed the direction of my life. I remember having a chat with Craig and my sister about growing up in a mainstream school and he understood exactly where we were

---

4   Fordyce, S et al "Post School Transitions of people who are deaf or hard of hearing" (2013) Research funded by the NDCS and conducted by Centre for research in Education Inclusion and Diversity

coming from. There were a few tears, because at last, someone understood what it was like, how hard it had been. I left that weekend a different person, so much more positive about my future and also with lots of new friendships which I still have to this day.

(Joanne Swinburne)

Nowadays, almost all deaf organisations around the globe offer 'deaf awareness' training to non-deaf people as a way of instilling empathy. At FYD the 3:1 ratio also offered 'hearing awareness' for people who had been brought up almost exclusively in a deaf society. The ratio enabled hearing people to develop empathy with deaf people:

The way that groups were chosen to make sure that Deaf people experienced what it is like to be in a majority gave me the insight to what it might be like for a deaf person in the hearing world as I was a hearing person in the Deaf world.

(Fleur Leslie)

With my unique experience as come from Deaf family I gained valuable experience to develop both hearing and deaf communities that lead me to build up confidence to be involve the real world which I found so tough after 16 years in deaf school and deaf family.

I found benefited the access into hearing world to learn the hearing culture that FYD taught me.

(Sylvia Simmons)

Life as a hearing person changed the day I joined FYD. It was a positive change and a change that I have always been thankful for.

(Pauline Collishaw)

Having attended Millfield in 1978, Dr Tilak Ratnanather says that the impact of FYD for him was an *"appreciation of diversity of deaf people"*. For too many young deaf people, their educational placements perpetuate the stigma of deafness, particularly around the stigmatising issues of sign language. Therefore it was important that our work on the philosophy of deaf/hearing integration was there to enable young people to understand and deal with stigma.

Yes! It was the first time I had ever seen deaf and hearing people working together on an equal basis without 'success' being determined by 'how good' the deaf person's speech was or how much the deaf person 'looked hearing'. That was a life-changing revelation to me and helped me shed my inhibitions with signing and to 'put to bed' the degradation suffered at my first school over my unclear speech and the constant brain-washing that 'signing people

Empathy (FYD)

look like monkeys'. I actually signed up on a Level 1 BSL course after my first FYD training weekend and discovered my deaf identity and how I could make things happen and achieve without trying to hide my deafness.

(Claire Ingham)

For the record, I want to say that FYD literally saved my life... as a young deaf person who attended mainstream schools (with PHUs) I was having a MAJOR identity crisis... at the time I hated the fact that I was deaf and feeling very ashamed and feeling angry at the world... and thankfully, people like Craig Crowley brought me out of a very dark place and introduced me to other-likeminded people who were deaf like me. I cannot underestimate how much FYD has done for me, and I am sure other people would agree.

(Helen Foulkes)

FYD was a life changer for many people including me. It inspired us to believe that we can be who we want to be without other telling us that we CAN'T.

(Damian Barry)

Looking back retrospectively, when I first got involved with FYD, I was on a dangerous path. I was becoming gradually more isolated as the communication in my school and family were becoming more complex. It wasn't possible for me to enter more challenging conversations if I couldn't hear them. In response, I was becoming more of a recluse. The work of Spivak applies to me here: she wrote about the subaltern, people who had no voice and were not expected to have one. By voice, I am not referring to the inability to speak, which was not the case for me, but the inability to be heard: to be heard as a person first and foremost. In the mainstream school, I was the 'deaf kid' – nothing more, nothing less.

In Birmingham and in company with like-minded people, I was suddenly not a subaltern any more. People wanted my company and wanted to create memories with me. Memory creating is an important part of growing up because they create shared myths, which results in a shared narrative and consequently a group identity. None of this could ever be created in the hearing world because communication, the central part of identity formation, was missing.

When I was travelling from Birmingham New Street to the venue, I was in the passenger seat and Damian at the steering wheel. The other passenger who was sat at the back leaned forward, quite precariously, so we could communicate with each other. I asked a question anyone would ask: "what do you do?" She said she went to University and signed in BSL with some lip patterns, which I picked up. I paused for a moment and spoke without thinking, "do you really go to university?" My question was loaded with misconceptions. My only defence was that those misconceptions were not my own; I had years of lies filled in my head. I was told that deaf people, who could sign, lived harder lives – they did not have the same opportunities as me and I was lucky to receive the education I had. Remember, I was miserable and terribly isolated, and yet, I should still feel lucky. And here before me was a deaf person, who signs, who is exactly where I wanted to be. I wasn't lucky; I was just manipulated.

Instead of sinking into the depths of betrayal, I started to ask questions: "so how do you cope at university?" Her reply was rather nonchalant retort at my naivety, "I have an interpreter." This was another omission from my education, no one taught me about how someone could sign, could also have access to 'human aids to communication'. I realised that no hearing aid, no communication gimmick could ever supersede the experience of communicating directly using the sense already available to me: communicating visually and manually. And that curiosity turned to hunger.

I lapped it all up; every sign; every joke and every moment to laugh. I learnt how not the isolate myself and began to bring others into the ever-growing group. As individuals we divided and colonsed, together we are united and a political voice.

(John Walker)

114

THE LEGACY OF FYD

Problem Solving: The ability to reason, use available information and think laterally in order to reach a goal or end point

The leadership weekends helped with decision making, finding solutions to problems and leading a team. I now run my own business with my sister Fiona and feel that my years of attending and being involved with FYD and all it's events and projects, laid the foundations for my future and gave me the confidence and self assurance that I have now.

(Morna Elliott, nee Rosie)

The biggest thing that did work with FYD was the 3 to1 ratio; deaf to hearing. This really allowed deaf young people to really feel like they were in the lead.

(Dr Tyron Woolfe)

Real-life lessons were learnt at FYD:

During one Bude team-building week I was involved in small group that had been dropped off in the middle of Dartmoor in terrible weather conditions with the task of navigating ourselves to a meeting point. We knew we had to look after each other, stay together and keep smiling.

The moment that will always remain with me was the disappearance of John Walker in a bog.

One second I was following him as he was using a compass – and then in the next, he was gone!.

I looked for him for a few minutes and then looked down, there he was shouting for help. We managed to pull him out. It made me learn that if you are in a situation like this, you have to stay positive, think rationally, support each other and stay calm.

(David Ingham)

The most significant barrier facing deaf people throughout their lives is communication and therefore being in a position to solve this is empowering. Our belief that communication was the greatest barrier to social inclusion, education and employment, is now backed up by research[5] – and our philosophy of Total Communication demonstrated itself as a problem solver when communication was organised and resourced correctly.

I enjoyed volunteering with FYD because of their philosophy – communication

---

5   University of Sheffield suggests that good communication is essential for transition to work or training, for independence and to access a range of life opportunities. Both the Rose Review and the Bercow Report highlighted the role of communication in attainment, and forming positive relationships. Improved communication skills have also been linked to reductions in reoffending.

Communication (FYD)

for all including deaf and hearing people to work together as one.

(Malcolm Sinclair)

Although I am profoundly deaf I had never personally experienced the problems faced by young deaf people because I was in my late 20's before I lost my hearing. Through going to the FYD sporting events, attending some of the excellent training courses and meeting the children and parents I started to see at first hand the difference that FYD was making. I remember being amazed at the ease with which deaf children communicated with their hearing siblings through sign language, and I determined to learn sign language myself – a skill that helped me enormously in my working life because it opened up the use of sign language interpreters.

(Dr Madeline Collie)

As a hearing person from a hearing family, I had never met a deaf person until I walked through the door at head office. I was keen to learn methods of communication to gain new friends and FYDs policy of Total Communication allowed me to learn at the same time as building friendships.

(Fleur Leslie)

The concept of Total Communication was introduced to me through FYD and its activities. Learning to sign was an accomplishment I might otherwise have never achieved.

(Jane Cole)

Communication is and always has been the key to making for a better understanding for everyone. FYD provided this.

(Marlene Swift)

Cooperation: Working together with others to the same end or goal.

Through working first hand with these young volunteers I was able to see how their confidence and organising skills developed; skills that stood them in good stead in later life when they were able to put them to good use in their careers, some of them have now gone on to important positions.

(Charles Herd, Deaf adult volunteer and later Development Officer)

I have a rewarding career in Information technology. It involves project management and developing software for a number of major government clients. FYD played a major part in developing my leadership ability and teamwork kills. Without these, I honestly believe I would be working in a

Co-operation (FYD)

poorly paid, dead end job.

(David Ingham)

The impact of the leadership taught me; the skills of two way communication and what the leadership role mean to us etc. Understanding and being mindful of the behaviour of others and being concerned for their needs, working out how to offer support and motivation and back up the people in my team. Skills of sharing ideas encouraging people to become decision makers rather than being a dictatorial leader.

(James Townsend)

Grit and resilience: Grit is the tendency to sustain interest in and effort toward very long-term goals. Resilience is the ability to bounce back

I remember on our way home from our first leadership course, we were at Derby station in the café. My sister Sarah went to get a coffee and the lady serving her was really rude to her, deliberately making it difficult for Sarah to understand her and then when she gave her change back, she slowly placed the coins in her hand one by one smirking.

Sarah was quite shaken by this, but as a result of this empowering FYD weekend, she went to find the manager and lodged a complaint against the waitress. She would never have done that before, but it goes to show, the immediate impact the FYD leadership course had on her straight away.

(Joanne Swinburne)

Resilience (FYD)

It was Morag who boosted me the most. I can't quite remember the exact words, but she said 'If you want something in life, you have to work hard to get it because no one else will get it for you.' Through goal setting with leadership training stages and various projects this gave me confidence to go out and get a job, get my qualification and training to where I am now today. If I did not go out there and get them, I would probably still be living life without them.

For me there are six important things that I have learnt from FYD: self-confidence, self-belief, leadership, conviction, humility and a can-do attitude. All of those things are still with me to this day. Without these, I would not be where I am now.

(Craig Crowley)

From the many projects and training courses, the mantra 'I can do anything' was instilled in me and is still with me today. The positive deaf role models inspired me and equipped me with leadership style to achieve results.

(Naomi Guest)

Bude holiday week helped me to overcome my personal fears and worries as well as making friends.

(Fleur Leslie)

Sense of Community: Identification as part of a community, perception of agency within it and propensity to take prosocial action

If I think about what I absorbed generally through being involved with FYD in the early days, it has to be about understanding that we are all on a journey of learning and development together. Hopefully progression! What my aunt Morag was passionate about was that the ideas of FYD should become much more mainstream and accepted in terms of attitudes and what deaf and hearing impaired young people and their hearing siblings, could expect from their lives. Both in terms of aspirations and opportunity but also about being treated as equals.

(Skye Holland)

My biggest memory of attending a typical FYD event was the yearly Crystal Palace events. I used to remember feeling nervous when arriving, and seeing all the different people of different ages, as well as mixing with deaf and hearing people. I used to remember seeing my Mum looking so happy mixing with her Deaf friends, and letting me do what I want to do.

(Yvonne Cobb)

FYD was important in introducing me to other deaf people of all ages and backgrounds and helped to reduce my isolation and increase my self confidence.

(Sarah Playforth)

Eternally grateful to FYD for the experience of friendship and the sense of belonging throughout my time with the organisation. Friends forever and a time filled with some of the greatest days of my life shared with the staff, volunteers and young people still remembered today. Even through I worked for the Midlands Embassy, I made friends from all over the UK through the National projects.

(Keith Wardle-Peck)

We were in an environment where communication amongst ourselves wasn't an issue. So we learnt how to be outspoken and confidant, and we learnt too, that when communication is not an issue, then we can be strong as people. We can put forward our views and not feel intimidated. It was an environment where we learnt about trust.

That helped me go forth into the world knowing who I was as a person. Also, backing me was a base of friends, whom I'd made through the FYD journey. So, I eventually ended up as a manager in my podiatry NHS department, and

A Sense of Community (FYD)

then went on to set up my own business locally so that I could juggle being a mum with working life. If I ask myself how much of my journey I credit to my formative years with FYD, I would say that it's a very large chunk. I had so much fun.

(Fiona Brookes)

The organisation had faith and trust in allowing me the chance to enter what I perceived to be a 'closed' community of people. They offered me the freedom to express my opinions and to offer these for shaping the activities and therefore the development of what FYD stood for.

There were challenges, which I needed to overcome such as how to effectively communicate with the varied and different types of languages used by deaf people. These challenges they helped me to face and overcome.

As a hearing person I was allowed to progress within the organisation and subsequently became a Regional Manager for the West Midlands. This gave me a greater insight into the organisations ability to reach out to deaf people across the country.

(Dennis Hodgkins)

I remember my weekend at Penn School learning to be leaders and working with the wonderful Damian Barry, being an inspiration I also remember getting in with deaf and hearing at conservation weekend having fun.

(Reg Cobb, CEO Gloucestershire Deaf Association)

My parents had always encouraged me to have belief in myself, but FYD allowed me to BE myself, in the company of others who really understood what being deaf was like.

(Jane Cole)

(As a 15 year old) I had identity issues; I was a deaf young lad from a huge deaf family and yet could hear quite well. I was not sure what my place was in the deaf community, and FYD gave me numerous friendships to explore these and find my identity.

(Dr Tyron Woolfe)

FYD has certainly played an important part in my life as it exposed me to the wider deaf community. It helped me realise that the community was where I belonged. At the events that the FYD organised, I made several new friends, built my confidence, learnt so many outdoor skills and was introduced to an immense range of sports. The most memorable impact that the FYD had on me was that it provided me with many adventures. It has certainly moulded me into the person I am today, a proud member of the Deaf community. I still

121

remain firm friends with some people who I met at Bude.

(Gavin Lilley)

What FYD brought for me – It took me to the other "world" away from my family & boarding school meeting other deaf people as well as hearing who sign. I didn't use sign language much at that time. It was amazing to see everybody of all ages and backgrounds. It was my first insight seeing other deaf people and sign language in much different context.

(Charlotte Moulton-Thomas)

Parents and children were surprised how much they had to offer, natural abilities and skills surfaced and friendships flourished in a warm and nurturing atmosphere. FYD provided our family with friendship and support and I am so pleased that we were part of an organisation that achieved so much for so many young people.

(Jackie Brookes)

My mother, Morag, was totally dedicated to integration between hearing and deaf people and believed that one of the ways to achieve this was through sport. The result now means that I can walk into my local tennis club, badminton club or others and I am immediately accepted because I have got something to offer them. The hurdles of being deaf are suddenly lowered and before you know it, you are an accepted member of the team. Of course, the communication barriers are still there to be broken down that can be achieved little by little.

(Fiona Brookes)

FYD made an important contribution to sustaining and building the network of the Deaf Community: Because projects and training programmes were held in different parts of the UK, the FYD programme enabled young people to travel and meet people they might not otherwise have met. Networking is very important for young deaf people, particularly as they often live in isolation. It was very beneficial for volunteers to meet at regional projects and be exposed to other cultures. Whilst hearing people may have instant access to information, deaf people need more first hand experiences to acquire a better understanding of things.[6]

Looking back, I can now say that I have come away from the self limiting, colonising education system and become the adept/bilingual person I sought to be. Once a friend put it in a nutshell "I was once an imperfect hearing person but now I am a perfect Deaf person.
    (John Walker)

6   P25, "Action Centred Development 1996-1999"

My first experience of FYD was an Initiative Training weekend in 1990, run by the legendary Craig Crowley. I made friends for life from that weekend and I still work with one of the other participants (who also trained as a Teacher of the Deaf), and have lunch in a nice café with her every week.

(Claire Ingham)

Educational Attitudes: Understanding of the value of education and taking an interest in building knowledge and skills

I realised that I needed to leave my comfort zone in Newcastle where my chances for new opportunities were bleak and followed the then Employment Minister, Norman Tebbit's advice that if you want to find work you have to get on bike and look for one – I did by writing to Morag that I would find one somewhere in London so that I would volunteer and take part in FYD projects under Morag's leadership.

(Craig Crowley)

I was 15, had attended Crystal Palace every year and wanted to do something "more" and be helping like "these deaf adults in front of me"... and then Damian Barry was introduced to me by Morag, and the rest is history!

(Dr Tyron Woolfe)

Educational Attitudes (FYD)

Nor was this skills and confidence building confined to the young volunteers. Working with them developed my own interpersonal skills which in turn stood me in good stead when I later studied for and gained a PGCE from Nottingham University and worked as a teacher at the City Lit in London and subsequently as a City and Guilds trainer on teacher training courses for deaf people.

(Charles Herd)

Deaf and Hearing Role Models

The unique proposition of providing deaf and hearing role models was the gel that enabled the intrinsic qualities to come together within individuals. For vulnerable young people and those from minority groups and communities, role modeling provides a spark and a catalyst of something that an individual can find from deep within and draw inspiration from.

It allowed me to develop my skills in an environment with like-minded peers, clear leadership from deaf role models, and the additional bonus of ease of communication; I could not have developed these skills with hearing peers whilst growing up.

(Dr Tyron Woolfe)

It was there FYD first introduced me to the world of self-confidence, self-esteem, self-awareness and opportunity to give it a crack at leading projects by example; after seeing so many Deaf role models during one week holiday coaching course there was this only person who did the unlocking of my potential – it was Morag Rosie, Director of FYD at that time.

(Craig Crowley)

Looking back to when I was younger and I went to FYD for different sports activities, football, athletics at crystal palace – these were simple things but they encouraged me I remember the wonderful leadership from deaf was amazing, Stuart, Morag, Craig, Chris Ratcliffe, Malcolm Sinclair, John Lewis, all those people, wow massive. Plus the blond haired woman, I cannot remember her name, she's disappeared, oh yes and Mandy Loach was another, all of them, these people were important figures, I think they were the influence on me."

(James Townsend)

… meeting several role models and overcoming my lack of confidence with my leadership abilities .
(David Ingham)

As leaders, we were there to lead by example and act as role models for what young deaf people can and should achieve in life. I was proud when youngsters

Tennis with Craig Crowley (FYD)

told me that we had made things special for them and that they had enjoyed themselves and wanted to come back, that they felt better in themselves for having had the opportunity that we gave them, that they wanted to go on the Leadership Weekends, that they, too, wanted to learn to develop themselves.

(Jane Cole)

I think the first person I met was most probably Damian – who was very confident, humorous and quite determined; it was not a quality I had seen in other deaf people within the limited exposure I had at the time. As a 17 year-old mainstreamer.

Sarah Cassandro Robinson from Redcar brought a lot of humour and I found myself laughing 'naturally and immediately' – something I had never done before. For the first time, I felt like a young person as a young person should feel. I also met Steve Crump, a very ambitious, energetic and slightly crazy army guy, who was slowly losing his hearing. If anyone had a misconception that deaf people could not be leaders, one would be damned to think otherwise in this place.

(John Walker)

Margaret Moore, was a volunteer with FYD until she moved to Carlisle in 1969 as the BDA Further Education and Youth Officer. She wrote in to comment about how important FYD was during a great period of development when people were starting to see more young deaf people entering further and higher education and training for sign language interpreters was becoming formalised:

> FYD was particularly important throughout these developments because of its vision and determination to involve so many young deaf people in its organisation and management. This enabled these young people to gain the necessary confidence to become leaders in their own right, to participate much more fully in all aspects of the adult world and to gain the respect and admiration so long due to them.

Personal Outcomes – The X Factor – Employability

Whilst we may have proven to some extent, that FYD provided opportunities for young people to discover and develop social and emotional skills, there has up until now been no research in relation to FYD to demonstrate whether these skills have been used successfully. Did FYD have the 'X-factor" to enable young deaf people to be more employable? Did the skills and knowledge gained from their time at FYD give young deaf people the resilience they needed to cope with the conflicts in life? Has FYD been useful?

We asked FYD participants to tell us where they are in their careers today and what influence FYD had on them. I will let them take us out from here to share the FYD legacy with you:

> Been involved since I was 7 years old (1987- Butlins) and it was the best thing my mom ever got me dragged into! When I was having some difficult teenage years, FYD was there like a superhero with all the activities available and now I am a youth worker – just to show that FYD could do to young people; with their motivation!
>
> (Claire Emma Fox)

> I still use the FYD leadership skills in my work as a Secretary now. I also used those skills as a Youth Worker in Middleborough Deaf Club and as a Deaf Youth Project Coordinator in RAD in London. FYD influenced me to be assertive, confident and to be myself.
>
> (Clare Perdomo)

> I would like to share how much I appreciated FYD training that does influenced both personally and professional since I joined Millfield Summer school aged 16 after left school in July 1979.
>
> After being training with leadership skills lead me full of potential to

open my self esteem and confidence to gain two degrees at Polytechnic and University I worked as assistant architect as full time and voluntary Youth worker with deaf young people.

Later with wealth of FYD taught me to lead my training to become a qualified youth worker with the British Deaf Association (BDA) and also involved Euro Youth Deaf Council in both role as Secretary and President till 1990.

After 25 years as youth worker I encourage Asian Deaf people and Newcastle young deaf people project which developed successful for 3 years and responsible BDA youth service. Later I move into rural youth service in Gloucestershire Deaf Association for short time then employed with Gloucestershire County Council Youth Service as Disability Youth Officer for 3 years.

During my time as a youth worker, I became involved in training others, so I moved into the field of education and trained as a teacher. I passed my PGCE with a Distinction to teach in adult education and then I became the co-ordinator with West of England Coalition of Disability then Social inclusion officer at Wales with British Deaf Association.

2007 I become Vice chair with British Deaf Association after many years as BDA paid staff to strengthen the leadership of BDA only deaf organisation.

Today I am now freelance as qualified general and mental health advocate in law setting to support the deaf rights to have access with their knowledge of information, access and communication in part of their human rights.

(Sylvia Simmons)

My FYD days have given me the skills of leadership and communication and I will continue to utilise these skills on a regular basis. I also gained empathy and understanding of the Deaf world, which, as a BSL interpreter is a vital skill.

(Fleur Leslie)

I work at Kings College Hospital London as a team leader for Health and Aging Unit. A lot of core knowledge and skills that I have learnt from the training programme are transferrable to my day to day aspects at home and at work.

(Naomi Guest)

My first involvement with FYD was in 1995 on the FYD Training programme. I have used their training methods in my own work as a BSL tutor and running deaf ethnic groups. They also gave me the confidence to run a group of deaf ethnic women in Luton.

(Parveen Dunlin)

Everything I have learnt at FYD still influences my work today; the expertise in training professional development and community engagement.

(John Walker)

I work as a design engineer for Airbus. I am also a governor for Heathlands School for the Deaf and I co-ordinate the Deaf Sports Personality of the Year. FYDs influence has helped my understanding in the area of leadership; quality, style, model, inspiration, vision and creativity. We re-launched the Deaf Youth Exchange under BDA with Switzerland, Japan and Russia.

(Richard Weinbaum)

We asked Richard to explain further :

At the time, I was involved with the British Deaf Association Youth section and they encouraged me to lead and re-launch the Deaf Youth Exchange with Switzerland in London before I departed for the USA. My lead was handed over to Tyron Woolfe (when the exchange went to Switzerland) and then to Angela Spielsinger/Oliver Westbury (exchanges with Russia and Japan). I was also involved with the 66 Club for ten years as a Sports Secretary, Event Organiser, etc.

We re-launched the youth exchange under the influence of one of FYD's aims where it broke down communication barriers between deaf/hard of hearing and hearing and international children/adults. The project was re-launched to foster international communication and intercultural dialogue, to empower our training and development to accept and deal with different opinions, religions and cultures by bringing Deaf, Hard of Hearing and International into contact with people from across the world. This built and developed cultural awareness; broke down social barriers and improved self-confidence through our leadership workshops, which helped us play a larger role in the future deaf/hard of hearing generation.

(Richard Weinbaum)

Today I work in the sports management industry. FYD has influenced my love for sport and they taught me so much. I am very grateful for that.

(Roanna Simmons)

I am a self-employed, confident, trainer, consultant. All the skills I learnt at FYD are still in use.

(Marcel Hirshman)

Through FYD, I decided to get involved with the British Schools Exploring Society and I went to Norway on a six week expedition in 1989 with the experience of FYD leadership training behind me. I had to learn to raise

Legacy : Surrey Deaf Youth Club Weekend (James Townsend)

a massive £3,500 to cover my expenses. I was still only 18 years old and at college but I managed to raise £4,500 to go on the expedition and buy the equipment I needed.

So where did all that come from? Was the influence from FYD? My next adventure was with Operation Raleigh when I was 22, we went to Guyana in South America and I was with a younger group of 17-18 year olds and I felt positive about myself as people looked up to me and were impressed.

Looking back from that time, all the influences from FYD coming to bear up to that moment in time, all the time slowly changing me.

It gave me the confidence to go to university 1990-1995 when, sadly, my involvement in FYD began to fade as I became more involved in my new life – but did all those early experiences still have an impact?

After university, I went travelling round the world for two and a half years, driving across the world travelling in different ways meeting so many people.

I was in Australia for one year and I got involved in football, golf and yes, I volunteered at FYD Australia! They were wicked times, with a guy called Doug. I supported their projects and Andrew Young when he was teaching leadership to others. I also got involved in a small project that was trying to develop young people.

When I got back to the UK, I set up CTS, Communication Through Sport, how did that happen? I met with Stuart Harrison, I arranged to talk to him because I wanted to do something that I could call my own project that was like FYD something that provided leadership for others. So I set up Surrey Deaf Youth Club (SDYC) and set up a camping weekend, which was focused around leadership, and communication skills that was down to the influence of the ideas of Communication Through Sport and Stuart supported by helping me with planning and organising. I got the funding, set up weekends, organised the activities and invited Stuart Harrison and Mark Perry to come along and help me to work with the participants and lead for one day on outdoor climbing and activities. Yes that was a great sense of success – gave myself another new belt of achievement.

The work I had done with SDYC gave me the confidence to apply for a job working in mental health; I was able to demonstrate my leadership skills and experiences. My employers were excited about the prospect of bringing leadership fundamentals to people who were living with mental health; organising their own events and activities and that all came from the experiences in my past looking back.

(James Townsend)

One part of the CCPR Sports Leaders Award was to complete few hours volunteering work. I volunteered at my old school to work on Saturday morning every week for some months. The PE teacher offered me to become his assistant sport coach. On Saturdays I had to encourage 50 young deaf boys to do 20 press ups, 10 sit ups and ran around the field in the coldest day of the month!! What a start of my teaching career!! The boys have remembered me ever since!

The school offered me a job as a sports coach working as an assistant to the PE teacher. He was remarkable man who was nearing retirement and he was still running 6 miles cross-country! This was the start of my career to become a teacher of the deaf.

(Malcolm Sinclair)

Career Influences of FYD:
- BDA Youth Exchanges – a great deal of responsibility, leadership and coordination
- Working with hearing team staff members – Civil Service Fast Stream Management Programme,
- University College London research
- PhD at Sheffield University – I think my FYD experiences enabled me to be very organised!
  I am the Deputy Director for children and young people at the NDCS.

Indeed FYD merged with NDCS for a few years before I came along. I am responsible for a team of about 21 staff (which was 6 when I started) focusing on Participation, Youth Activities and Inclusion. We work with huge numbers of deaf children and young people and everything I have learned from my days in FYD holds very true in this role. Indeed the views and thoughts of deaf children and young people has really shifted NDCS from being parent-focused to that of child-centered.

(Dr Tyron Woolfe)

In the early to mid '80s I attended a series of Management and Leadership Training courses, what I learnt on those weekends of enjoyment I use in my work when I am facilitating workshops in drama and sign songs.

(Caroline Parker MBE)

Some people changed careers after joining FYD:

FYD provided me with the skills to progress into a professional career in sports development, this I remain grateful for.

(Dennis Hodgkins)

I was involved in the leadership training having spent 12 years working in Admin and thinking that was what I would be doing for the rest of my life, I never thought I would be able to do a job as a Development Officer with FYD, and loved every minute of it and meeting so many new people, setting up projects and giving something back to all those that started out like me.

(Sharon Smith)

In 1990 at the age of twenty one I looked at Ceefax pages and I learnt about Initiative Training course held at Dukes Barn. At that stage of my life I was working in a Residential Home for the Elderly in Cardiff.

At that point in my life I had a very limited social life. I already grew up feeling isolated at school being the only Deaf pupil at the local high school. I had to cope in the absence of a Teacher for the Deaf with what should have been my formative years. I left school learning very little to show for it. The lack of achievement did not do anything good for my self worth or self esteem.

It is because of FYD that I became a Youth Worker. I have been a Trustee of the British Deaf Association. I am Chair of Cardiff Deaf Sports and Social Club and a Trustee of Cardiff Deaf Centre. One thing I did was to achieve the Certificate of National Examination Board of Supervisory Management. I wanted to others to know that I have both not only the experience but the qualification to match it.

(Stuart Parkinson)

The testimonial above reminds me that it has been good to hear how former participants have continued to use and refer to the FYD project manuals and training manuals in their working lives. It is good to see that they do indeed have a have a long shelf life AND are still in use! Stuart Parkinson still uses the project manual in his work and its effectiveness was echoed in the complements he received on how well a recent Arts Festival was run at the Cardiff Deaf Centre.

After FYD, as always, I searched for new ways to help young people to experience new opportunities which saw me besides teaching and coaching swimming other sports, I was approached to assist with setting up and running a new Youth and Community Centre in Bradford. I qualified as a Youth Worker and in a part-time capacity I was at Greenwood for 18 very happy and rewarding years until retirement age. I also took my City and Guilds working as a volunteer at Skipton College teaching the 3 R's to adults with learning problems. All this and more working full-time in various departments at Bradford and Bingley Building Society sadly now no longer functioning.

(Marlene Swift)

Some people have built a career around the principles of FYD:

I first joined FYD on the volunteering scheme after a year of trying to become employable through youth training schemes. At FYD I felt valued in the workplace and not stigmatised.

I took my experiences to work at Crystal Palace Sports centre and then a stint as a retail shop manager. But I went back to FYD and opened up the opportunities with the British Schools Exploring Society.

I know that I got a place at university on the back of my work experience with FYD, this was a far stronger attribute than my qualifications at the time.

For my teaching career and beyond to date; the fundamentals for me have all been about developing opportunities to establish the FYD principles of deaf and hearing partnerships and the Adair principles of leadership.

(Stuart Harrison)

I always wanted to be a teacher and FYD gave me the confidence to do it. Working with FYD taught me that there is a solution to every challenge and gave me the opportunity to work with young people from all walks of life, so, I appreciate how life experiences influence our life choices and attitudes; something I've always been aware of in my teaching.

(Claire Ingham)

For what it is worth – I still carry FYD around with me wherever I go. I just sow the seeds. I don't preach it, I just act on it and people start to see that they can

President Barack Obama greets Dr. John Tilak Ratnanather, 2012
Presidential Award for Excellence in Science, Mathematics and Engineering.
Mentoring (PAESMEM) recipient, The John Hopkins University, in the Oval
Office June 17, 2015. (official White House Photo by Pete Souza)

reach their full potential. I have been doing this here in Northern Ireland and slowly we are seeing a growing pool of trained people who potentially will be leaders of the future. This is what it is all about.

(Damian Barry)

For others, the legacy of FYD has been about social action and giving back time to the community:

I am deeply involved in my charity 'Children of Deaf Parents UK' I have used what I have learnt from FYD to ensure this charity 'ship' is running smoothly. It is still going strong after 10 years, believe it or not! I am also a parent Trustee of my son's football club.

(David Ingham)

I am doing cutting edge research at one of the top 15 universities in the world. What I have taken away from FYD is the benefit of mentoring. I have mentored five deaf or hard of hearing undergraduates – all who have gone into medicine and now are qualified physicians. In addition, I have created and lead a cohort of deaf and hard of hearing people all over the world who do research in auditory sciences.

(Dr Tilak Ratnanather)

The Impact of FYD on my immediate family:

I remember the early weekend projects that we used to go to at Romney Marsh and Millfield and again I now realise that when most kids were trying to find things to fill their weekends, ours were totally full, If not on a project, then at the stables with my family.

We started to provide accommodation at our house for the new volunteers that started to influx (or so it seemed!) in to our lives. This was a massive period of adjustment for me as I'm sure it was for my dad as well as mum and, I'm sure, for the volunteers themselves.. Most coming down from the north to the south! A massive culture shock!

The first of the volunteers, Craig Crowley, came, all bright eyed and bushy tailed! Fiona and I together with Mum, soon licked him into shape. Cooking and cleaning is definitely a mans job as well as a woman's! After Craig, more young people came through our door. At one point, mum and dad had to put a few of them up at the bottom of our garden in a garden house!

The one person I haven't really mentioned is my lovely dad Hamish. He's been the backbone of the family, as it is said; behind every great woman is a great man!! Through all of these events, changes and invasions, he kept smiling and never grumbled. My poor long suffering dad even had to spend a lot of his weekends at the stables (he really didn't like the horses) mucking out, fetching giant hay bales and saw dust from the local sawmill with my uncle George … filthy job! Again, he never grumbled and just got on with things … I'm sure he felt it was the only way he'd get to see the ladies in his life!

(Morna)

FYD formed a huge part of my early years. I saw it grow, as a young child, from its first seeds to an organisation that was managing some form of project virtually every weekend. Being the daughter of the director had its perks, and I was able to attend a huge variety of projects, mainly sporting and sometimes art. These weekend and week-long activities gave me such a fantastic opportunity to try my hand at different sports.

(Fiona)

I will let others have the final words:

Thirty seven years later I am forever grateful FYD asked me to part of it that led what I am now successfully part of contribution to all walk of Deaf diversity, young people, ethnic minority, family and elderly I gave them all the positive

"Thank you" (John Wheeler)

and happy in the Deaf community.

Simple to say thank you Friend of Young Deaf you are always part of my life.

Thank you and God bless you all who I met you all and make my friendship fruitfully.

(Sylvia Simmonds)

I would like to thank all my colleagues at that time for such a wonderful journey but most of all the people who made it work from the office staff to managers but my biggest thanks go to the volunteers who came in and gave their time relentlessly to support the vision of FYD without them my work and the work of FYD would not have been so successful.

(Keith Wardle-Peck)

So thank you to all the unsung heroes that are part of FYD. Thank you for changing my life for the better but most of all thank you Morag. If it wasn't for your encouragement, I would not have plucked up the courage to leave Newcastle to take up the post in FYD.

I wouldn't be where I am now.

(Craig Crowley)

9

Is FYD Still Relevant Today?

When requesting testimonials, one of the prompts we gave was: "Is FYD still relevant today? Yes or No, why?" because I wanted to understand why people still think that FYD should be "brought back" for the benefit of current and future generations of young people.

The analysis of the responses that we received illustrated that the philosophy of FYD is still relevant and that the NDCS has developed some of the practicalities of the FYD programme it inherited. But there are other things missing that will help to enable young deaf people to develop social and emotional skills in the context of the 21st century.

> … the world today is a very different place for young deaf people, with so much more emphasis on inclusion and the advance of cochlear implants and other technology. FYD gave me knowledge (of other deaf people), leadership skills and self-confidence – I cannot believe that there isn't still a place for those qualities today. I'm so glad my childhood, adolescence, young adulthood had FYD in it and I wouldn't change that for the world.
>
> (Jane Cole)

> More relevant than ever because … Reduced facilities at schools and the austerity regime of this government may mean young people cannot easily afford to get involved in sports or other activities.
>
> (Sarah Playforth)

> FYD is as relevant today as back then: if not more so as more and more Deaf People are being employed in a professional capacity and even running their own businesses.
>
> (Caroline Parker MBE)

> The philosophy of 3:1 was good and probably would still work today. Technology would be our hardest battle if we tried to revive a similar model to FYD.
>
> (Marcel Hirshman)

> "The absence of FYD, the increase in cochlear implantation and mainstreaming

combined with cuts in support means that deaf children are now facing even more challenges. Through my work at NDCAMHS[1] I have seen a noticeable increase in deaf children who are in crisis over their identity."
(Dr Hilary Sutherland)

The National Deaf Children's Society

What I am certain about; is that the NDCS activity programme for deaf children and young people is a faithful continuation of the FYD participation projects which are lead by teams of deaf and hearing staff/volunteers. There are elements of training on offer for young deaf people and the BUZZ website created in collaboration with young deaf people, promotes opportunities for social action. There is strong evidence to show that the legacy of FYD does indeed survive within the NDCS; as my good friend Susan Daniels, NDCS Chief Executive explains:

I first became involved with FYD in the late 1980s during my time as a lecturer in deaf education at the City Lit Centre for Deaf People.

My involvement in FYD gave me huge respect for the work that FYD was doing to increase the skills and confidence of young deaf people, and improve communication and understanding between deaf and hearing young people.

When financial difficulties threatened FYD's viability, as CEO of NDCS, I was extremely keen to consider ways in which my organisation could support the continuation of FYD's work. After much discussion between the two organisations a merger followed in 2001.

At that time, most of NDCS's work was targeted at parents of deaf children through information advice and support services.

After the merger between FYD and NDCS, we ran a number of activities for deaf children. In 2007, NDCS set up a separate division focused solely on working with deaf children and young people, and appointed Tyron Woolfe as its Deputy Director.

NDCS then undertook the largest ever consultation with deaf children and young people (DCYP) across the UK, with more than 1,400 responses, which directly influenced our work in this area.

Every deaf child has the right to the same opportunities as a hearing child, yet many leisure organisations are not fully accessible. Through the NDCS Deaf friendly football and swimming projects as well as our Me2 activities, providers are taking small and simple steps to turn themselves into genuinely inclusive organisations for deaf children and young people.

NDCS runs a UK wide youth activities programme for 8-15 year olds to participate in multi-sport and creative activities that build their confidence and give them the opportunity to learn new skills in a deaf friendly environment. Trained deaf people (role models themselves) who work for NDCS on a

---

1   National Deaf Child and Adolescent Mental Health Service

sessional basis are employed to run sessions with the children.

We encourage deaf people to become role models to younger children. We have many deaf volunteers, a good number have volunteered with NDCS as a result of their childhood experience of NDCS.

For the sixth year running, we continue to run our Young Leaders programme. Deaf young people aged 16-18 works towards an accredited course in sports leadership, undertaking some theory and then leading activities for the children's programme. They are taught by deaf tutors who have a background in sports coaching.

With over 1,800 members, DCYP have benefitted from opportunities to engage with others on-line and get information first hand, read stories about other inspiring DCYP and find out more about NDCS and non-NDCS events up and down the country.

NDCS has invested heavily in developing deaf children and young peoples ability to influence the NDCS. We have a thriving Youth Advisory Board (YAB) with 18 members from all over the UK. The YAB have developed information and advice resources, peer support, consulted with young people about things that matter to them e.g. audiology services, deaf youth-led campaigns, e.g. Look Smile Chat, My Life My Health. The awareness that has been achieved in wider society about the views of DCYP has been hard work and challenging, including a young deaf person meeting the Prime Minister!

(Susan Daniels, Chief Executive, National Deaf Children's Society)

Despite the good news about the ongoing work of the National Deaf Children's Society, perpetuating the legacy of FYD, there are still people who benefitted from the original FYD who believe more still needs to be done:

FYD is missing from today, even though other organisations that provide opportunities to children and young D/deaf people are around, I still don't feel they offer the same as FYD did to the young D/deaf people who have I have crossed paths with and who I feel would benefit so much from what FYD offered.

(Sharon Smith)

If the question is 'What is missing?" then the collective understanding from the testimonials is that there is a need for carefully designed programmes that enable a working partnership between deaf and hearing people, and also something that caters for deaf and hearing participants over the age of 18. Allow me to explain:

The partnership between deaf and hearing people

The philosophy of integration between deaf and hearing people is still relevant.

(Naomi Guest)

Now that cochlear implantation of deaf babies is freely available, the challenges that they will face during childhood are different from those that faced deaf children 30 years ago. But the FYD philosophy of friendship and understanding between deaf and hearing people is still valid, so it is good that people are still talking about this small organisation that had such a big impact!

(Dr Madeline Collie)

The most outstanding and unique offer from FYD until shortly after the merger with the NDCS, was the inclusion of non-deaf children, young people and adults into the programmatic activities that were also embedded within the staffing structures. The 3:1 ratio of deaf and hearing participants across all programmes was a deliberate strategy, designed to create optimum conditions for inclusion/integration to work. Our intention for this policy was to give both deaf and hearing people the opportunity to experience and learn from the impact of integration and develop empathy of each other, in order that they could create a more equitable society together. Damian Barry was able to explain this very well during an interview in New Zealand when he was asked if FYD was based on getting deaf and hearing people together:

That is the fundamental principle. We bring together Deaf and hearing people on a 3:1 ratio of three Deaf and one hearing. That allows the comfort zone for Deaf people to come together. It also allows hearing people to experience what it is to be in the minority but in a very positive environment. To go into a minority situation where there is no support mechanism is disorienting for many people. We provide a supportive environment for hearing people to understand what it means to be in a minority. When they go back out into the community they are aware so they can bring the Deaf people into their own community.

(Damian Barry 1997)

FYD did not champion this partnership because of the impacts of different education philosophies (with mainstreaming and segregation as the two extremes). We advocated the deaf/hearing partnership regardless of whether a deaf child comes from a deaf or hearing family or whether or not their schooling is mainstreamed or segregated, because they all have to develop a life-balance of deaf and hearing friends to enable them to succeed and get on in the hearing world.

Whilst adult role models working together gives young people a sense of the potential possibilities for their own lives, they have no way of testing out their own abilities to form friendships and relationships in an environment that is safe and controlled. It is for this reason that it is important to run activities for deaf and hearing participants together.

The FYD experience of being in a reversed-integration situation (3 deaf participants to every hearing one) where deaf people can blossom and succeed is a unique one and is key to developing young deaf people's belief that they can achieve and influence the world around them.

(Claire Ingham)

Catering for participants over the age of 18

A right pity is the loss of leadership and management training courses for older young people.

(Dr Tyron Woolfe)

The FYD programmes did not stop when people reached 18 years of age. Indeed, if I look back at our work, the greater majority of young people who became members of staff or significant leading volunteers on our activities were all aged 17-18 years old, or more, when they first encountered FYD.

Their contemporaries who joined FYD at a much younger age, whilst still at primary or secondary school had been able to make better decisions about their transitions by the time they reached 17 or 18 years of age. One of the reasons for making successful transitions was the opportunity to share a common experience with hearing peers of their own age, combined with the benefit of deaf/hearing adult role models.

I still feel in today's society Deaf Young People need adult role models and training to become more confident and self efficient. Hopefully one day the National Training Programme will return to prepare the next generation. Right now I am organising an Arts Festival which I could not have done without my past experience thanks to FYD.

(Stuart Parkinson)

The importance of providing somewhere for young people to turn to in their 20s and 30s can be illustrated in the story of Claire Ingham, who had begin to make a successful start to her career, but when events turned for the worst, she needed somewhere to go:

At the time I was a research post-graduate student at Durham University and was feeling increasingly isolated, especially after one close friend moved to another University far away and then my closest friend was killed in a car crash and I plunged into a depression. My social life disappeared and I was finding it harder to make new friends amongst the other, hearing, researchers (my two close friends had been really easy to communicate with and we went along to social events together, even holidaying together. Thanks to an old school friend who encouraged me to try FYD Initiative Training, I found a new

140

direction in my life, made new friends around Middlesbrough and Newcastle and became involved in setting up NEAT (the North East Action Team) which involved running projects locally as part of a very enthusiastic, dynamic – and fun – team.

Claire eventually decided to postpone her place on a PGCE course when we offered her the post of National Projects Officer. She re-started her teacher training after she got married and completed her teacher of the Deaf training over the same time period as having her two children! Following a very successful career as a Teacher of the Deaf, specialising in literacy, she is now self-employed as a supply teacher. She assesses and supports deaf and dyslexic students, teaches deaf adults, provides tutorial support to university students and provides tailor-made training courses around deaf literacy for organisations and services.

A 21st Century approach

A new format National Leadership Training programme and Action Centred Development is needed for older young deaf people aged 18+ with the proviso that the new interventions are delivered in a context that is more suited to the 21st Century.

> In this present time, it (FYD) really is even more relevant: everything in society, it seems, is in a state of flux. For anyone – perhaps more so for young people – this is truly unsettling and fearful. FYD could be that rock, that safe harbour, which can be relied upon – always.
>
> And it can, more positively, look at, discuss, new thoughts and activities. Build upon what FYD did – develop it further in so many different ways, for example, self-advocacy.
>
> I discovered, through being a Member of the GLC/ILEA and an education charity I set up, just how lacking in self-confidence many young people are; and how essential this is for, not only individual success, but success for those sometimes overlooked.
>
> (Edna Mathieson)

> The proliferation of cochlear implants and digital hearing aids has facilitated a significant increase in mainstreaming in recent years. However, problems such as noisy classrooms, which can affect cognitive processing, make mainstreaming sub-optimal. Focusing on confidence building and problem solving exercises should be at the heart of FYD activities. Anything else is too consequential or incidental.
>
> (Dr Tilak Ratnanather)

I agree with Alison Bryan, a veteran of over 50+ FYD events and courses when she says that something of the old FYD could be revived but we have to accept that it would not be the same. She quoted Heraclitus *No man ever steps in the same river twice, for it's not the same river and he is not the same man.*

Earlier this year (2015), Rob Wilson, the Minister for Civil Society spoke at a Cabinet Office event about 'Youth Social Action'. After reading the original script[2] of his speech, I am now more convinced that the services that were offered by FYD still have a place in today's society and would provide the much needed missing gap in service provision for deaf and other vulnerable children and young people. What Wilson had to say is as relevant today as it was when Denis Uttley first started. In the script of his speech, the minister reinforced the drive behind *Youth Social Action*, and when you understand what it means, you will agree with me that it was also the very essence of FYD.

> Our young people being the change they want to see in the world. Our next generations developing the skills and gaining experience they need to fulfill their potential. Our communities benefitting from great projects that enrich their local areas. Social action brings out the best in young people.
>
> (Rob Wilson MP, 2015)

Government ministers, service providers and commissioners of interventions for young people have dug out various pieces of evidence that show that deaf, disabled and other vulnerable young people participated in social action programmes such as the Youth Parliament, National Citizens Service, Step Up to Serve and Uniformed Youth. On the basis of this, the majority consensus is that these transition programmes are inclusive because there is evidence that young deaf people are taking part. But I suspect that the outcomes and outputs are not being examined in terms of young deaf people and 'inclusion' is not working in the way that it should because the missing ingredients are not being applied. Attempting to include young deaf people into mainstream interventions for 18-20 and 20-30 year olds will fail, if providers fail to acknowledge and act upon the following:

- If we want to equip deaf young people to operate successfully in today's society we need to recognise the needs of both deaf and hearing and meet their needs
- To continually separate deaf and hearing people does not help break down barriers that exist between them
- To advocate 'integration' without proper preparation and support is counter-productive
- To train deaf and hearing people together, on an equal basis, befits both parties

---

2   Rob Wilson on youth social action – https://www.gov.uk/government/speeches/rob-wilson-on-youth-social-action

- Communication needs of all participants need to be addressed and supported
- Theoretical learning has to be complemented by experiential learning
- Deaf young people are particularly well qualified to help others, with appropriate support.

(Evaluation of the Action Centred Development Programme, 1996-1999 p38)

The most frustrating thing of all occurs when the evidence of good practice of partnership between deaf and hearing people is put before decision makers. It is provided in the form of third party reports and other media sources – established after the fact. So, unless decision-makers can experience something for themselves, it really does not have a personal impact on them and so a change in decision-making doesn't occur. We have to create more opportunities for young deaf and hearing people to be together in the right environments, if we want to see change in the future.

> FYD gave many people, including myself, the opportunity to develop themselves or engage in "personal development". I believe that the success of FYD was in the creation of opportunities where the deaf people who participated had a realistic chance of working through the process of building up self esteem and learning leadership skills without the additional difficulties of communication experienced in situations involving people with normal hearing and potentially lacking in deaf awareness. By working through the process of learning leadership skills in controlled, sympathetic situations, the deaf participants stood a far better of dealing with the challenges thrown at them in normal situations later on in their lives.
>
> (Dr Hamish Drewry)

The experience of being with deaf and disadvantaged young people is necessary – this is why it is important that all organisations who provide programmes for deaf children and young people should factor in the involvement of non-deaf peers from the outset. This way there is a greater chance that those experiences will influence decision makers when they are older and have agency themselves. Marlene Swift, who was with me in the early years at East Grinstead and developed the *sports festivals* concept, gives a very good testimonial of what professionals miss by not being immersed in effective environments of deaf/hearing partnerships.

> During my working and recreational life it has been an amazing conclusion that other than being involved with FYD I would not have experienced and witnessed the problems that the hearing impaired are confronted by in their every day lives.
>
> (Marlene Swift)

Closing Time

During the course of writing this book, I was asked how I felt when I received the news from the FYD Trustees of their decision to close our offices and merge. Naturally it was hard to accept that it had just happened and it was a big thing for me to accept the end of FYD's, unique, 30-years of service.

But this journey of writing with Stuart and looking at the whole thing from the first day of my involvement with FYD to the time of my retirement, I know that I achieved my aim of creating opportunities that supported the development of young deaf and hearing people.

To me, it had been a 30/40-year long pilot and we have been able to see its impact 14 years after we merged with the NDCS. I believe that the programme worked because we did prepare young people to reach the end of their training with the ability to make decisions about what they wanted to do with their own lives, either in readiness for employment or in continuing education at a college or university of their own choosing. But it has taken 15 years since the merger to see this. I hope that this book will enable everyone to understand the impact of FYD from those who were fortunate enough to go through the National Leadership Programme and move on in their personal lives and careers. Sarah Playforth has reflected on what FYD achieved and has expressed this beautifully in a short poem:

Seeds sown with care and love
Grew and flourished in ground watered and nourished
By people who knew the way to show
Young people how to find their own path.
Such blooms emerged – sturdy and bright -
Sowing seeds of their own in the FYD light.

I am proud of what I have achieved as a profoundly deaf person. The process of writing this book, has forced me to look at myself, jogging along over the years alongside the FYD philosophy, I know that the reality of my dream came true. The recognition of my work when I was awarded the MBE in June 1991 is still a recognition that I want to share with everyone who has ever been involved in FYD. I said at the time that I was very pleased about the award because it gave credibility to the work and efforts of FYD so that people would recognise the importance of what we tried to do. The whole process, the seeds sown by Denis Uttley, the establishment and development of FYD, its merger with the NDCS and the fourteen years since have all been the most wonderful 'pilot project'.

We have also created a fleet of 'drivers' from all over the country and abroad who, based on their experiences with FYD are now concerned about the present generation of 18 – 32 year old deaf and hearing young people and their readiness for a life that contributes meaningfully to society. We are all keen to see the development of something new that would be appropriate for the present and

Hamish and myself at Buckingham Palace for my MBE, 1991. (FYD)

future cohorts of young people.

I end here thanking the most important person to me, who has stood by me through the years behind all this. Hamish, my dear husband, has been my rock, supporting me in different ways all the way along through those thirty years. As an exhibition display designer and artist, working at the Greater London Council, he helped as a volunteer with the designs of FYD literature and newsletters. Not only this, he developed our Art projects and Exhibitions. Thank you Hamish, I owe you a depth of gratitude for your lifelong support.

Postscript – Garvel School

Whilst my sister and I did not benefit from a good education at Garvel School, I was pleased to discover in a journal of the British Deaf History Society,[1] that, after 1976, sign language was introduced as the method of instruction in Garvel after one teacher commented, "These children are being sacrificed to a system."

Martin Colville from Moray House College of Education provided "Visual Communication" classes for staff and parents and in May 1977, the school was using the term "Total Communication" imported from the USA.

The Garvel approach to Deaf Education began to attract national interest and visits from experts working in the field of sign language overseas (Scandinavia, Holland and the USA), the school was also a subject of some TV programmes. In the decades that followed, the school evolved further to ensure that children were developing their language skills through BSL where it was needed.

Today, the Garvel Deaf Centre is based in Moorfoot Primary School, Gourock where the children have an inclusive education, spending sometime in both specialised and mainstream classes. There is also a peripatetic service attached to the centre for children who require less intensive support.

We wish everyone at Garvel all the very best for the future.

---

1   British Deaf History Society, Deaf History Journal, Autumn 2012, Vol 15 issue 3.

Lightning Source UK Ltd.
Milton Keynes UK
UKOW06f2316211015

261145UK00002B/2/P